GREAT MYSTERIES

Shamans

OPPOSING VIEWPOINTS®

D1709460

Look for these and other exciting *Great Mysteries: Opposing Viewpoints* books:

GREAT MYSTERIES

Shamans

OPPOSING VIEWPOINTS®

by Wendy Stein

Greenhaven Press, Inc.   P.O. Box 289009, San Diego, California 92198-0009

Library of Congress Cataloging-in-Publication Data

Stein, Wendy.
   Shamans : opposing viewpoints / by Wendy Stein.
     p. cm. — (Great mysteries)
   Includes bibliographical references and index.
   Summary: Discusses that intermediary between the human and spirit
worlds which still exists in some societies performing rituals,
healing, and seemingly possessing extraordinary powers.
   ISBN 0-89908-088-X (lib. bdg.)
   1. Shamanism — Juvenile literature. [1. Shamans.] I. Title.
II. Series: Great mysteries.
BL2370.S5S83 1991
291—dc20
                                           91-14498

To my parents
Doris and Harold Stein

Contents

Introduction

This book is written for the curious—those who want to explore the mysteries that are everywhere. To be human is to be constantly surrounded by wonderment. How do birds fly? Are ghosts real? Can animals and people communicate? Was King Arthur a real person or a myth? Why did Amelia Earhart disappear? Did history really happen the way we think it did? Where did the world come from? Where is it going?

Great Mysteries: Opposing Viewpoints books are intended to offer the reader an opportunity to explore some of the many mysteries that both trouble and intrigue us. For the span of each book, we want the reader to feel that he or she is a scientist investigating the extinction of the dinosaurs, an archaeologist searching for clues to the origin of the great Egyptian pyramids, a psychic detective testing the existence of ESP.

One thing all mysteries have in common is that there is no ready answer. Often there are *many* answers but none on which even the majority of authorities agrees. *Great Mysteries: Opposing Viewpoints* books introduce the intriguing views of the experts, allowing the reader to participate in their explorations, their theories, and their disagreements as they try to explain the mysteries of our world.

But most readers won't want to stop here. These *Great Mysteries: Opposing Viewpoints* aim to stimulate the reader's curiosity. Although truth is often impossible to discover, the search is fascinating. It is up to the reader to examine the evidence, to decide whether the answer is there—or to explore further.

"Penetrating so many secrets, we cease to believe in the unknowable. But there it sits nevertheless, calmly licking its chops."

H.L. Mencken, American essayist

Foreword

The Mysteries of Shamanism

In the Canadian Northwest Territories, a shaman travels to the spirit world to help his people...

The Iglulik shaman sits silently behind a curtain in the inner part of his tent. He wears only boots and mittens. He breathes deeply for many minutes. Then from out of the silence he calls his helping spirits: "The way is made ready for me; the way opens before me." He repeats the words over and over again. And each time, the people assembled outside the room answer, "Let it be so."

The spirits arrive and the earth opens beneath him, but only for a moment. There is not enough time for him to pass through. He struggles with the hidden forces until finally the earth opens again and he cries, "Now the way is open."

The people answer, "Let the way be open before him; let there be way for him." Cries of "Halele-he" come from behind the curtain. The shaman continues to call out and his cries come now from under the ground. His cries become fainter and fainter. When the people no longer hear his voice, they know he is on his way to see Takanakapsaluk, the Sea Spirit. She has withheld the sea animals and hunting is bad. The community is afraid it will

(opposite page) North American Indian shaman in full ceremonial dress.

> "We are so accustomed to the apparently rational nature of our world that we can scarcely imagine anything happening that cannot be explained by common sense."
>
> Psychologist Carl Jung

> "The world is not only that [which] we see. It is enormous and also has room for people when they die and no more walk about down here on earth."
>
> Nalungiaq, Netsilik Eskimo shaman

starve. The shaman must convince Takanakapsaluk to release the animals into the upper world.

Ordinary shamans may encounter dangers on the way to the spirit's house. Three huge stones at the end of the passage roll around and threaten to crush anyone who passes through. A fierce dog guards the palace of Takanakapsaluk.

This shaman is a great shaman, however. Great shamans pass without obstacles. He glides through the earth as if it were a tube. It is fitted to his body. He can slow his progress just by pressing against the sides. The spirits keep the way open for his return.

The shaman reaches the Sea Spirit's home. The house has no roof so she can watch humanity. She is angry. She sits with her back to her lamp. She also ignores the sea animals—the seals, walruses, and whales—lying in the pool of light next to the lamp.

Meeting with the Sea Spirit

Her hair hangs loose and tangled, hiding her eyes. The misdeeds of the people are dirt on her body. The stench of their sins nearly choke her. The shaman turns her around to face the lamp and the animals. He combs and strokes her hair. Finally, when she is calmer, he tells her the people above are unable to catch any animals. Takanakapsaluk answers by reciting the broken taboos and sins of the community.

The shaman soothes her anger. She is feeling kinder, so she picks up each animal and drops it on the floor. A whirlpool arises for each one and the animal disappears into the sea. The shaman can now return to his home.

The people above can hear him from a long way off. The sound of his passage through the tunnel gets closer and closer. Then with a great gasping for breath, he shoots up into his place behind the curtain.

There is silence until he speaks. "I have something to say." The people answer, "Let us hear, let us hear." But he is silent. His silence forces them to confess their broken taboos. After all has been confessed, the people are joyful. The hunt will be good.

Crystal Power

In Australia, a Kurnai youth becomes a shaman...

Tankli dreams his father and many older men tie a magical cord of whale sinew around his neck and waist. They swing him by this cord and he lands in the other world in front of a huge rock. There is an opening in the rock. His father blindfolds him and leads him inside. He hears the rocks moving behind him as he enters. When the blindfold is removed, the place is bright and all the old men are seated there.

His father points to the shiny rock crystals that cover the walls. He tells Tankli to take some. Tankli takes one and holds it tightly in his hand.

They leave the crystal room and go outside. His father teaches him to put the crystals into his leg and pull them out again.

His father and the old men carry him back to the camp and put him on the top of a large tree. As instructed, he shouts that he is back. The people wake up. The women beat their rugs for him to come down because now he is a *Mulla-mullung,* a shaman.

Tankli awakes to find himself sleeping on a limb in a tree. When he comes down he finds he is still holding the crystal. He tells the old men all that has happened and they tell him he is now a Mulla-mullung.

Now, he can heal people. He knows how to pull out of people the things that cause sickness.

Helping the Dead

In Siberia, a Goldi shaman escorts a soul to the Land of the Dead...

A man has died many weeks earlier and it is time for his soul to travel to the Land of the Dead.

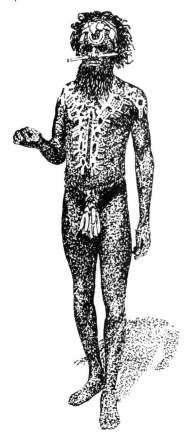

Australian aborigine shaman with distinctive body paint. The drawing on his forehead represents the shaman's hand—his instrument of power.

The dead man's friends and relatives gather for a banquet.

The shaman puts on his costume made of animal skins and decorated with feathers, animal pelts, and sacred symbols. Beating his drum, he searches for the soul near the yurt (tent). He dances and tells of the difficulties there will be along the road to the underworld. He finally captures the soul and takes it inside the tent. He puts it in the *fanya* (a cushion). The banquet continues late into the night. When it is time to sleep, the shaman tucks the fanya in bed and tells the dead person to sleep. Then he sleeps, too.

The next day, he wakes the dead with his drumming. There is another banquet and at night he puts the fanya to bed again. This may go on for many days and nights. At last, the shaman announces it is time. He sings, telling the dead person to eat well because the trip will be long and hard. At sunset, he gets ready to leave. He sings and dances. He rubs soot on his face so the spirits of the dead will not recognize him. Then he asks his helping spirits to help him and the dead one's soul on their journey to the beyond. The shaman climbs a notched tree and

Shaman of an extinct Californian Indian tribe and examples of his tribe's artwork.

scans the land for the road to the underworld. When he finds it, he comes down and returns to the yurt.

With dancing and singing and drumming he summons his two helping spirits. This shamanizing leaves him exhausted. Now he sits down on a board, which is his sled for the trip. The fanya and a basket of food are beside him. The spirits harness the dogs to the sled. A spirit servant accompanies him and they set off for the Land of the Dead.

As he speaks to the servant, the people of the village follow the journey through his words. The road becomes more and more difficult. There is a great river that only a powerful shaman could cross.

When the shaman sees footprints, ashes, and bits of wood, he knows the village of the dead is nearby. Soon, he hears dogs from the village, and sees smoke from the yurts. The dead gather and ask who the shaman and the newly dead are. The shaman does not give his real name or he may not be able to leave. He looks among the crowd for the relatives of the soul he brings. He entrusts the soul to them.

Now he hurries back to the land of the living. And he tells how the dead one is doing in his new home. He also brings each of the people messages from the dead relatives.

And then he throws the fanya into the fire.

One

Shamanism: An Ancient Tradition

Shamans are travelers and explorers in a world most other people do not see—the spirit world. In a trance state, these men and women can journey to the spirit world. The shaman's soul leaves the body behind and travels freely in the sky or through the earth.

"All at once I was way up there with the birds. The hill with the vision pit was way above everything. I could look down even on the stars, and the moon was close to my left side," says Lame Deer, a Sioux shaman.

"When people sing, I dance, I enter the earth. I go in at a place like a place where people drink water. I travel in a long way, very far," says African shaman, Old K"xau.

Masters of Ecstasy

The word shaman comes from the word *saman,* from the language of the Tungus people in Siberia. It means "one who is excited, moved, or raised." That is a good description of shamans. They are often said to be in an "ecstatic state" when they work. Ecstasy means "moved out of one's self." It is a state of intense joy. Mircea Eliade, a religion historian, calls the shaman a "master of ecstasy," because the shaman's soul, free of the body, can fly

(opposite page) An American Indian medicine man dressed in a bearskin performs a healing ceremony.

freely anywhere. Shamans can journey, whenever they choose, through time and space to distant parts of the earth or even to other worlds.

Old K''xau says, "When you go there, friend, you make yourself small like this. . . . You come in small to God's place. You do what you have to do there. Then you return to where everyone is. . . . You come and come and come and finally you enter your body again. . . . You enter, enter, enter the earth, and then you return to enter the skin of your body . . . and you say he-e-e-e. That is the sound of your return to your body."

Shamans "travel" by going into a shamanic trance, which is a different state of awareness than

Painting of paradise by sixteenth-century Flemish artist Jan Brueghel. Most human-origin legends tell of people living in paradise in harmony with gods and animals. Usually, humans are evicted from paradise. Humans can no longer talk with animals and gods, and so require an interpreter, such as a prophet or a shaman.

the normal waking state. In the shamanic trance, shamans are able to explore or ask for help on behalf of their people. They seek reasons for a person's illness or hunt for a lost soul or power. They search for the reasons for a poor hunt or look to see what is in store for their people. Many shamanic people believe the events and activities of the spirit realm cause the events in the physical world, including death, sickness, the weather, and the supply of food and water.

How Shamanism Began

Shamanic people have their own beliefs about how shamanism started. Long ago, according to many traditions around the world, the earth was a paradise. People could easily communicate with the heavens. They could even travel physically to the spirit world. According to the stories of the Koryaks of Asia, people could reach the sky by climbing through a central opening in it or by following the path of an arrow shot upward. In Japan, Polynesia, Indonesia, and other places, a rainbow bridged the sky and the earth. Still other stories tell of a ladder, tree, pole, or rope that connected the three worlds.

The stories tell that a rift occurred between the gods and humans. People no longer lived in this easy paradise. Then there was sickness and death and hardship. The gods sent a "first shaman" to help humans. Among the Finns and many Siberian peoples, the first shaman was an eagle. In one version of the story, the gods told the eagle to give the gift of shamanizing to the first person it saw. The first person the eagle saw was a woman, who became the first shaman on earth. In other stories, the first shaman was born of an eagle or was trained by the eagle to take "magical flights."

The Iglulik Eskimo shaman Aua tells a different story. Even in the earliest times, there was sickness. At first, people healed each other. "Everyone was a physician, and there was no need of any shamans."

Knud Rasmussen, half-Eskimo, half-Danish arctic explorer, talked to many Eskimo shamans during his explorations.

But then there came a time of severe hardship and famine. Many people died. The people did not know what to do.

One day, they gathered in a house. One man hid himself behind the skins hanging at the back of the tent. He announced that he would ask the Mother of the Sea Beasts for help. No one believed him, but he said he knew how to do something that would be of great value to all of humankind. He said they must not watch him. Before long, however, people grew curious. They pulled aside the hangings just in time to see the man diving into the earth. "He had already gone so far down that only the soles of his feet could be seen," Aua relates. "How the man ever hit on this idea no one knows. He himself said that it was the spirits that had helped him: spirits he had entered into contact with out in the great solitude. Thus the first shaman appeared among men."

The Decline of Shamanic Powers

The early shamans in most traditions were very powerful. They retained their power for many generations. Like the shaman in Aua's tale, they could travel physically to the spirit world. They could change themselves into animals and birds. Carib (Dutch Guiana) lore says that early shamans could see spirits with their physical eyes and could bring the dead back to life. Perhaps the shamans became too proud, for the stories tell that the gods or God punished them. The gods cut off their direct, physical access to the spirit worlds. From then on, only the spirit self could travel while the shaman was in a trance.

According to stories of peoples around the world, the decline of shamanic powers continued through the ages. An Eskimo shaman told explorer Knud Rasmussen in the 1920s: "I am a shaman myself, but I am nothing compared with my grandfather Titqatsaq. He lived in the time when a shaman could go down to the Mother of the Sea

Beasts, fly up to the moon, or make excursions out through space."

Religion historians and anthropologists (people who study human culture) tell a different story about the beginnings of shamanism. Some experts trace shamanism all the way back to the beginnings of religion on earth.

Anthropologists guess that religion was a very early development among humans. They guess that a belief in an afterlife is at least one hundred thousand years old. They base their conclusions on evidence found in prehistoric caves in Europe and Central Asia. In a cave in France, archaeologists found the remains of a Neanderthal child. His body had been placed as if asleep with his head resting on his arm on a "pillow" of flint shavings. Near him were animal bones and tools. It seems as if his tribe believed these things might be useful to him in the next life. And if the people believed in an afterlife, this also means they believed that some part of the dead person survived—a soul or spirit self.

Edward Tylor was a British anthropologist working in the late nineteenth century. He guessed that the belief in a soul and an afterlife came from dreams. Prehistoric people must have believed that a dream self traveled to a dream world while they slept. Death also seemed like a deep sleep. So, once people could conceive of two separate selves and a dream place, it was a short step to these next beliefs: The soul could travel outside the body, and there was another world beyond death.

Animism

Religion historians also guess that at this early stage, people may have begun to think that all things had spirit—animals, plants, even rocks. Tylor called this belief *animism.* The word comes from the Greek word *anima,* meaning soul.

In an animistic world, all things have soul or spirit. All things have personality. And all things are related. There is a kinship among all beings and things—humans, animals, and even the earth itself. Everything in the animistic universe is sacred because it is alive and it is a relative. But because everything is alive and has life energy, everything also has power. This grand network of power can be overwhelming and dangerous to humans. They must always be careful not to anger or offend any of the spirits. For example, every animal killed in the hunt has a spirit, and that spirit just might seek revenge. An Iglulik Eskimo shaman told explorer Knud Rasmussen: "All the creatures that we have to kill and eat . . . have souls, souls that do not perish with the body and which must therefore be pacified lest they should revenge themselves on us for taking away their bodies."

So someone was needed to act as an intermediary between humans and spirit beings. A person was needed who knew how to exercise control over the mysterious powers that ruled the universe.

Shamanic Paintings

Prehistoric cave paintings with shamanic overtones have been found in France and northern Spain. These shamanic paintings are fifteen to seventeen thousand years old. But they are painted over other thirty-thousand-year-old paintings. This suggests that the caves themselves had supernatural importance. It suggests that people were performing religious ceremonies in them at least thirty thousand years ago. Those ceremonies may have involved shamans or some kind of supernatural figure.

One of these famous cave paintings is found deep within the Lascaux caves in France. Dated at about seventeen thousand years old, it is painted on a wall in a lower gallery that is accessible only by a rope ladder down a six-meter shaft (about twenty feet deep). The painting depicts a bison with an arrow through it. It faces a man who lies on the ground, either dead or in a trance. Near the man is a

"Archeological . . . evidence suggests that shamanic methods are at least twenty or thirty thousand years old."

Shaman and anthropologist Michael Harner

"Since archeological interpretations must so often rely on analogies with contemporary primitives they are not always conclusive. There is justifiable reason for being cautious in using archeological data to say that the art of the Upper Paleolithic is magico-religious in nature."

Anthropologists William Lessa and Evon Z. Vogt

Among the earliest known works of art, this wall painting discovered in a French cave depicts animals and shamans dressed as animals.

pole with a bird on top of it. Some experts say the painting depicts a hunting accident. But others believe that the man is in a shamanic trance asking the gods for a successful hunt. In many cultures, the bird-pole stands for the magical or soul flight of the shaman.

A painting from about the same period in France's Magdalenian caves shows a man wearing a bird mask and holding a bird staff. According to mythology expert Joseph Campbell, this staff is similar to shamans' staffs all over the world.

A fifteen-thousand-year-old drawing from the Les Trois Frères caves in France depicts an animal-like figure. It has the antlers of a deer, the face of an owl, and the long tail of a horse. This painting seems to suggest that prehistoric people believed in magic. Shamans and magicians are believed to be able to change themselves into other creatures. Experts say this is probably a drawing of a magician who changed into an animal. This drawing may be related to hunting rites.

These ancient cave drawings depict part of shamanic practice even today—the ability to change into an animal to communicate with the spirit world.

The Role of the Shaman

As shamanism developed, shamans came to perform several important functions for their communities. In cultures ruled by the supernatural, their work is vital to the people's well-being.

Healer. Shamans are "medicine people." They heal members of the community. In shamanic belief, the cause of illness is found at the spirit level. It is loss of soul or power or the intrusion of an enemy spirit. The shaman must communicate with the spirit world in order to diagnose the problem. Then the shaman travels to the other world to bring back the soul. Or the shaman removes the intruder by sucking it out.

All shamans are healers. But not all medicine people are shamans. To be shamans, healers must work in the spirit realm.

Intermediary. Shamans are supernatural diplomats. They carry requests to the spirit world. They return with instructions from the gods. The Iglulik shaman who visits the Sea Spirit or Mother of the Sea Beasts is acting as an intermediary.

Psychopomp. Psychopomps are conductors of souls. As psychopomps, shamans accompany the souls of the dead to the spirit world to help make them comfortable. As "masters of the spirit world" or "masters of death," shamans teach their people about the world of the dead. They make death familiar to them so that it will not be so frightening a transition when they die. The Goldi shaman of Siberia who guides the dead to the underworld is working as a psychopomp.

Shamans work for the good of the community or individuals. But the journey also helps keep the

Renowned expert in world mythologies Joseph Campbell noted the many similarities between shamans around the world and throughout history.

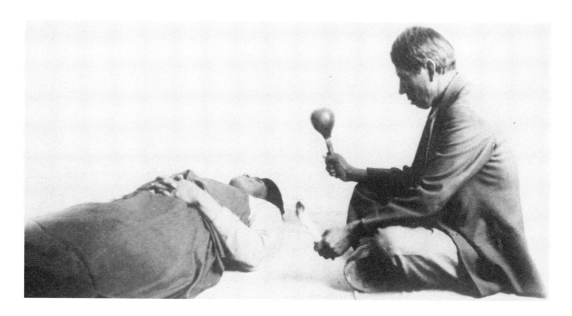

shamans healthy. Many shamans report that when they do not perform shamanic rites for some time, they begin to feel ill.

The shaman is a figure of great power and wisdom. Manuel Córdova-Rios, a shaman, was trained by an Amahuaca shaman of the Amazon in South America. Córdova-Rios describes the old shaman: "I remember wondering how old this man might be. Actually, his physical features did not give the usual signs of age. . . . Nevertheless, he gave the impression of being ancient. . . . He maintained a calm, distant aloofness from the people and their activities, yet gave the feeling of complete awareness of present, past, and future events. And one felt that their awe of him was justified."

Despite their awesome powers, shamans do not consider themselves greater than anyone else. Powerful shamans are usually quite humble. North American shaman Lame Deer observes: "Seeing me in my patched-up, faded shirt, with my down-at-the-heels cowboy boots, the hearing aid whistling in my ear, looking at the flimsy shack with its bad-

A Papago Indian shaman from the American Northwest uses a rattle and deer tail. These items will help the shaman enter a trance and send healing power to the sick person lying before him.

smelling outhouse which I call home—it all doesn't add up to a white man's idea of a holy man. . . . You know I'm not better or wiser than other men. But I've been to the hilltop, got my vision and power; the rest is just the trimmings."

The Decline of Shamanism

Historically, shamanism began when people still lived in hunting and gathering communities. These were communities in which people hunted animals and gathered wild plants rather than cultivating food. The shaman was the spiritual leader.

As people began to settle down and to farm, communities became larger and more complex. A fixed order began to develop. Institutions such as governments and religion arose to keep the order. Religion became more organized. Specialists took on many of the shamans' duties. Healers specialized in the use of herbs or other methods. Priests emerged as the leaders of organized religion.

Priests did not deal directly with the spirit realm as the shamans did. The priests' work was based on supernatural events of long ago. The priests were chosen by the religious organization, not directly by the spirits. They did not travel to the spirit world. They followed a set format. They memorized words and ceremonies.

Author Roger Walsh, in *The Spirit of Shamanism,* points out that in complex societies all of the shamans' functions except one were taken over by other specialists. That function was "journeying," the very activity that is the basis for shamanism.

Michael Harner is a shaman and anthropologist. He suggests that shamanic religion has been suppressed by organized religion because it is dangerous. It threatens the authority of the state church. Shamans interact directly with the spirit world. They are beyond the control of the church because their power comes directly from a supernatural source.

Shamans were killed as witches and wizards

Modern-day shaman Michael Harner is also an author and anthropologist.

during the Spanish Inquisition in the 1500s. Traditional shamanism was practiced in northernmost Europe among the Laplanders until the 1930s. Then Christian missionaries forbade the use of the drum. The drum is one of the most important tools of shamans. Its beat helps them enter their shamanic trance.

Growing belief in science and "rational thought" also influenced the decline of shamanism. Before science, people explained nature in terms of supernatural forces. Science developed rational explanations for rain and disease. Science explained away the mysteries that had once awed people. Belief in science replaced belief in the supernatural. Shamanism almost disappeared except in isolated pockets around the world.

Shamanism Around the World

The similarities in belief and methods of shamans around the world are remarkable. For example, dismemberment or replacement of organs by the spirits during initiation occurs in Siberia, South America, North America, Africa, and Australia. Caves play an important part in initiation in South and North America, Australia, and the Arctic.

Shamanism is still practiced in parts of Siberia, North America, Mexico, South America, Africa, Australia, Indonesia, Southeast Asia, and Asia.

Siberia. Siberia is the home of "classical" shamanism. That is, the very definition of shamanism is based on the tradition practiced in Siberia.

Shamans in Siberia are healers and masters of ecstasy, journeying to the sky and the underworld. Siberian shamans rely on the steady beat of the drum to help them enter their trance state. They wear traditional ornate animal costumes and headdresses. They dance to "transform" themselves spiritually into these animals. They are also considered masters of fire. They are able to handle red-hot coals without being hurt. They heal both by retrieving lost

"A sophisticated Westerner tends to consider the belief in an afterlife and the concept of the posthumous journey of the soul as products of primitive fears of individuals who have been denied the privilege of scientific knowledge."

Medical researchers Joan Halifax and Stanislav Grof

"The problem is that the Westerner is simply unsophisticated from a shamanic point of view."

Anthropologist Michael Harner

souls and by sucking out the spirit intruders.

North America. Shamanic practice is found among Alaskan Eskimos, as well as among the Tlingit people of the Pacific Northwest, the Paviotso of western Nevada, the Chiricahua Apache of Texas, Arizona, and New Mexico, the Lakota Sioux of Dakota, and the Nez Percé, Ojibway (Chippewa), Zuni, and Twana people.

It is not surprising that the shamanism of the North American Eskimos is similar to Siberian shamanism; they live close by and in similar conditions within the Arctic Circle. However, the

A shaman from northern Siberia poses in full costume with his drum.

shamanism of the Paviotso of Nevada is also very similar to that in Siberia. Paviotso shamans enter trances, and, while in spirit form, they retrieve lost souls and cure people. They also perform ceremonies to affect the weather. Among most other North American people, shamanic practice is common, but it may be difficult to tell the difference between shamans and other holy people because roles and practices have been absorbed and combined.

Mexico. Shamanic culture is still very strong among many native Mexican people, including the Mazatecs, Chinantecs, Zapotecs, and Mixtecs. Sacred plants that induce visions and trances are plentiful in Mexico. They are commonly used as part of the shamanic practice.

South America. There are many kinds of spiritual practitioners in South America. There is not always a clear difference between shamans and *curanderos* (medicine people). South American spiritual roles have been influenced by African and Christian practices as well as folk practices. Like Mexico's shamans, South American shamans commonly use sacred drugs to induce the shamanic trance and visions.

Africa. Strong shamanic elements are evident in many African cultures. For example, !Kung shaman Old K"xau describes diving into the earth as the Siberian shamans do. However, shamanic practice and belief is often interwoven with other healing and magical traditions.

Australia. In Australia, the shaman is known as a Mulla-mullung or *karadji* ("clever man"). Shamanism on this continent is usually much less ornate than in Siberia. The only costume may be a few body paintings. Many accounts tell of the karadji leaving their bodies to see events far away. Like Siberia's shamans, they also travel to the spirit world, which they call Dreamtime. And like Siberian shamans, they are said to be able to handle

Apache medicine man sits with his magic staff while an assistant beats a drum to induce the shaman's trance.

A shaman in Bangkok, Thailand.

hot coals without being burned. Australian shamans also use musical instruments to help them enter a trance. Healing is usually by sucking extraction rather than retrieving a lost soul.

Indonesia. In Indonesia, shamans go into trances and spirit travel. In Borneo, the Dyaks call the shaman a *manang*. The Menangkabau of Sumatra call the shaman a *dukun*. New shamans have visions that are similar to the visions of shamans in nearby Australia and faraway Siberia. Spirits cut open the shaman's head and wash the brain. Magical substances are inserted in the body to enhance the shaman's powers.

Southeast Asia. Shamanism is still practiced in Southeast Asia, especially among the Hmong people of Thailand, Laos, Vietnam, and parts of China. Refugees from these countries have carried shamanic practices to their new countries. The Hmong shaman is called the *Txiv Neeb,* the "father/master of spirits." The Hmong have a relationship with the supernatural and perform many healing rites themselves. But for serious problems, the Txiv Neeb is called upon to enter the spirit world to rescue captured souls or intercede with the nature spirits. The shamanic tradition is central to the Hmong view of the world and is a link to their past. Hmong shamans in the United States and Thailand have no problem using supernatural techniques along with modern medicine, herbs, or massage to heal the sick.

Asia. Shamanism or traces of shamanism still exist in parts of Tibet, China, Japan, Nepal, and Korea. In isolated villages in Japan, female shamans called *miko* enter trances and communicate with gods and spirits of the dead. The Tamangs of Nepal practice shamanism that also has some elements of Hinduism and Buddhism. In China, the shamanic influence is found in Taoism.

Shamanism and Technology

Today, a resurgence of shamanic techniques can be seen among people in modern technological society. That is due largely to the work of Michael Harner. Shamanism "is our common human condition" and our common human past, he says. It does not belong to the East or the West or only to the native peoples around the world. It belongs to all of us. After all, humans have believed in science for only a few hundred years. They have believed in the supernatural for tens of thousands of years, says Harner.

Two

What Is the Shaman's Reality?

The shaman's reality is hidden from ordinary sight. It is invisible except to people with the "strong eye"—spirit vision. María Sabina, a Mazatec shaman, says of the other reality: "There is a world beyond ours, a world that is far away, nearby, and invisible. And it is where God lives, where the dead live, the spirits and the saints, a world where everything has already happened and everything is known. The world talks. It has a language of its own. I report what it says."

The shaman sees into the secrets of the universe. Sabina says, "Millions of things I saw and knew. I knew and saw God: an immense clock that ticks, the spheres that go slowly around, and inside the stars, the earth, the entire universe, the day and the night, the cry and the smile, the happiness and the pain."

Nonordinary Reality

Anthropologist Carlos Castaneda calls the shamans' hidden world "nonordinary reality." Shamans are able to move freely between nonordinary reality and ordinary reality. It is this ability to travel back and forth that makes them shamans.

Anthropologist Åke Hultkrantz writes: The shaman "exists in two worlds: outside the trance he

(opposite page) Mazatec shaman María Sabina speaks of what she sees in the invisible spirit world while in a trance.

lives the daily life of his tribesmen; inside the trance he is part and parcel to the supernatural world, sharing with the spirits some of their potentialities: the capacity to fly, to transform himself, to become one with his spirit helper."

The spirit world is as real to shamans as this world is to us. The spirit world, or nonordinary reality, has trees, lakes, oceans, rivers, meadows, souls, and spirits. To shamans, it is all real. It is even more vivid, more vibrant, than what most people experience in ordinary reality.

States of Consciousness

Shamans gain access to the other reality through a trance state, an altered state of consciousness. They learn to control their states of consciousness during their training period.

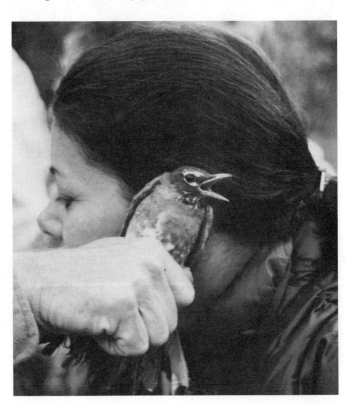

A student listens to the heartbeat of a bird. In the world of the shaman all creatures, even stones, have souls.

Consciousness is what a person is aware of at a given time. Consciousness could be compared to a TV set. The set receives signals transmitted from another source, a TV station. TV viewers can tune into the signals from only one channel at a time. If they want to watch another show, they must change the channel. Then they can receive the signals from another source.

Michael Harner calls the normal awake state of consciousness the "ordinary state of consciousness" (OSC). People spend most of their waking hours in the OSC. They are tuned into the physical world in which they work, study, and play. To gain access to another reality, they must switch to another channel, an altered state of consciousness. Everyone experiences altered states of consciousness. Sleeping, dreaming, and daydreaming are altered states. Other common altered states are experienced during hypnosis and meditation. People also enter altered states when they take drugs.

A Shaman's Journey

When shamans "journey," they are in an altered state. They are "tuned into" the spirit world. Shamans are able to switch "channels" very quickly. Or maybe they are in more than one state of consciousness at the same time!

According to Harner, the shaman "might tell you of splitting a large tree at a distance with his shamanic power, or that he saw an inverted rainbow inside the chest of a neighbor. In the same breath, he might tell you he is making a new blowgun or that he went hunting the previous morning." In other words, to the shamans, all that they experience is reality. They do not see any boundaries between ordinary and nonordinary reality. They do not stop to think, "this belongs to the spirit world, and that to the physical world."

Harner calls the shaman's awareness the "shamanic state of consciousness" (SSC). The

"When presented with something we believe to be unreal, we doubt our senses or our sanity."

Mary Schmidt, anthropologist

"Shamans are taught as soon as possible that the objective world is only one way of seeing."

Serge King, anthropologist

depth of this trance state varies among shamans of different cultures. For example, among many North American shamans, the trance is very light. Åke Hultkrantz says, "A shaman may seem to act in a lucid state when, in actual fact, his mind is occupied with interior visions." Some shamans even narrate their adventures as they travel in the spirit world. In other instances, the shaman seems to be unconscious or even dead. Among the Lapps of the Arctic Circle the trance is so deep, the shamans appear to be in a coma. But when they return to ordinary reality, they remember everything that has happened to them.

The SSC is an "ecstatic" state. Shamans experience great joy and awe when they encounter the beauty and mystery of the spirit world. That is why Mircea Eliade calls the shaman "a master of ecstasy."

The Soul

Shamans explain it is the *soul* that journeys. *Soul*, *consciousness*, *life force* and *spirit* may all be words for the same idea. The soul, free of the body, is very powerful. It is not limited by time or space. It is part of the oneness of the world and therefore is capable of knowing everything.

Shamans value the soul above the physical being. Utkuhikjaling Eskimo shaman Ikinilik says: "The only thing of value in a man is the soul. That is why it is the soul that is given everlasting life, either in the Land of the Sky or in the Underworld. The soul is man's greatest power; it is the soul that makes us human, but how it does so we do not know. Our flesh and blood, our body, is nothing but an envelope about our vital power."

Shamans are in great danger when they leave their bodies. This condition leaves the empty body in a deathlike state, and the soul is in danger from spirits or enemy shamans. Safe return to the body is essential for the shaman's survival. Old K"xau says,

"He-e-e-e. That is the sound of your return to your body. Then you begin to sing. Then *n/um k"xausi* are there around! They take powder and blow it . . . in your face. They take hold of your head and blow about the sides of your face. This is how you manage to be alive again. Friend, if they don't do that to you, you die! . . . You just die and are dead." (*N/um k"xausi* are his power and healing energy.)

Most people's souls travel even while they are alive, according to shamanic belief. The soul is said to leave the body during sleep, dreams, serious illness, or after a bad accident. It might even escape during a sneeze. Most people cannot control the wanderings of their souls. Shamans, however, are powerful because they can choose to leave their bodies. They are masters of soul travel. Once trained, they travel at will while their bodies lie in trance in ordinary reality.

The Shamanic Structure of the Universe

The soul can journey anywhere in the universe. According to shamanic belief, the universe is made up of three main levels—upper world, lower world, and middle world. In some cultures, there are several levels of the upper and lower worlds, sometimes nine or more. The upperworld is the realm of the stars, the moon, the sun, the gods, the ruling spirits, and the souls of some of the dead. The lower world is the world of the souls of the dead and the spirits of illness. The middle world is the earth, the world in which we live.

The upper and lower spirit worlds do not take up physical space above the sky or below the earth. They are not made up of solid matter and cannot be reached with the physical body. But, free of their bodies, shamans are able to leave ordinary reality and journey to these spirit worlds.

Shamans enter the lower world through a hole or opening that acts as a doorway between the

"[In contemporary science] there is no more uncharted space left for celestial spheres, hierarchies of angels, or God."

Stanislav Grof and Joan Halifax, medical researchers

"I am inclined to believe there is more to the universe than the human mind."

Michael Harner, anthropologist

worlds. Knud Rasmussen reports that Eskimo shamans of Hudson Bay claim that a hole opens up in the earth or sea ice for the descent to the lower world. The shaman's spirit passes through the hole and along a road or tunnel to the otherworld. Shamans also enter the underworld through caves, animal holes, hollow tree stumps, or whirlpools. Some Australian shamans claim to dive into the ground and come out again wherever they choose. Anthropologist Franz Boas in the early 1900s reported that the Bellacoolas of the Pacific Northwest had a hole in their homes between the doorway and the fireplace. This hole was an access hole for the shaman to enter the underworld. The *kivas* (ceremonial chambers) of the Zuni people of the American

A *kiva*, a sacred room built half underground, has a hole in the floor where the Pueblo Indian shaman can enter the earth while in a trance.

Southwest have a hole in the floor for entrance to the underworld.

Shamans ascend to the upper world from a raised area such as a mountaintop, treetop, or cliff. Or they may fly on the back of a bird, especially the eagle. Shamans can ascend to the heavens by fire or smoke. Or they might climb a mountain, a rope, a ladder, or a rainbow that connects the three worlds. The Tsimshian of Canada drill holes in their totem poles for ceremonial access to the heavens. Australian shamans say they climb to heaven on a thin thread that comes out of their mouth. Others climb a rope that is invisible to ordinary humans. For some Eskimo shamans, a hole in the snow hut opens, "a hole like the blowhole of a seal." In North and South America, there is a legend of a "chain of arrows." The shaman shoots arrows into the skies, making a chain between earth and heaven. The shaman can ascend to heaven with the help of this chain.

Landscapes of the Spirit World

Descriptions of the actual landscape and beings of the spirit world are as varied as descriptions of the earth. But many descriptions resemble our world—with a slight twist. The lower world may be a shadow or an inverted (upside-down) version of earth. For example, to the Samoyeds of Siberia, rivers in the spirit world flow backwards, the tips of trees grow down, and the sun rises in the west. Life begins with old age and the souls of the dead get younger and younger until they are babies ready to be born again. When the hunt is poor in the middle world, it is good in the lower world, and vice versa. In some tribes, people leave broken objects on graves so that the objects will be whole in the land of the dead. To the Yukagir of Siberia, the lower world is a shadow version of the middle world. The shadow spirits hunt shadow animals and live in shadow tents.

Painting of an American Indian shaman going into a trance after shooting arrows into the sky to create a "chain" of communication with the spirit world.

The upper world is often a grander version of earth. Everything is richer, more luxurious, and more plentiful. Plants may flower all year long. There is no death, pain, or suffering.

Even the middle world is different for the shaman, who is able to see the true nature of all things. Everything in nature has spirit—mountains, rocks, trees, flowers, animals, and people. The shaman is able to see the spirits and talk with them. According to the Hopi of North America, in the human world all creatures and plants are in disguise when most people see them. But all of these creatures have the same "spark of life" that humans have. In fact, their spirits all have other homes in which they live in human form. Shamans can see them in their real form.

The Axis of the World

The three worlds are linked by a central axis called the Axis of the World. The axis passes through a hole in the earth to reach the lower world and a hole in the sky to reach the upper world.

The central axis is considered the center of the world because it is the sacred place through which gods, spirits, and shamans can pass. But the spirits and shamans can pass through at many different places. So there are really many "centers of the world."

The central axis is portrayed in many ways. Shamanic people in Central and Northern Asia see the central axis as a World Tree or Tree of Life. The tree's roots are in the lower world, its trunk in this world, and its branches in the upper world. According to religion historian Mircea Eliade, the tree gives life. It stands for the life and growth of the universe.

Some Siberian people believe the souls of children who will become shamans are perched in the branches of the tree. The higher the child-soul is perched, the greater will be that shaman's power. Shamans visit the World Tree during their training. It is said that Siberian shamans' drums are made from the wood of the World Tree.

The central axis that links the worlds might also be a cosmic mountain, a river, a rainbow, a bridge, the World Pillar, or the Pole Star. (The Pole Star is also called the Sky Nail or Nail Star. You may know this star as the North Star.)

The World Pillar or Pole Star holds up the sky as if it were a tent. The other stars are holes for light. The central poles in the traditional dwellings of many people of the Arctic, North America, Central and North Asia, and Africa symbolize this cosmic structure. Sacrifices are often placed at the base of the pole. The smoke hole at the top of some tents or huts lets smoke out. It also stands for the hole through which shamans and spirits pass between the earth and the upper world.

Is the Spirit World "Real"?

Most scientists doubt the existence of this spirit world. If it is a world of energy or spirit, why does it have "form" like this world? They also find it suspicious that this other world is so similar to ordinary reality. Certainly, they say, it must come from the shamans' own imagination.

Shaman expert Holger Kalweit suggests that the shaman's vivid descriptions of the spirit world resemble this world only because the shaman uses this world for comparison. Humans can "picture" it only in terms of what they already know. The spirit world is really beyond description. Trying to describe it is like describing "wet" or "cold" to someone who has never known wet or cold. The shaman tries to translate the mystical into terms people can understand.

Not all of science is skeptical of the shamans' reality. One branch of science offers another possible explanation for the spirit world's existence. Its theory would also explain why the spirit world looks like this world. The Many Worlds Hypothesis of modern physics presents the possibility of "parallel universes." According to this hypothesis there are other realities that "branch off" from the one we know. Each of these realities is a parallel universe. Physicists explain that parallel universes are the worlds "that might have been." The number of other possible universes is endless. Each universe represents "possibilities" that did not come to be in this world. They are the worlds of "what if?"—What if this person was not born? What if the chemistry of the world were slightly different? What if everyone who has died lives together somewhere else?

"Experimental studies in psychology have shown that mental imagery can become so vivid that it can block out the awareness of normal visual perception. It is almost as if the vibrant world within becomes so bright that it blocks out the light from the world around one."

Richard Noll, psychologist

"Observation with one's senses is the basis for the empirical definition of reality; and there is no one yet, even in the sciences of ordinary reality, who has uncontestably proven that there is only one state of consciousness valid for firsthand observations."

Anthropologist Michael Harner

Eskimo drawing depicting a person's guardian spirits.

Perhaps shamans see these alternate "realities." When they travel, maybe they visit these other worlds.

Spirit Helpers

Shamans are accompanied on their journeys by their spirit helpers. Explorer Knud Rasmussen learned from Eskimo *angakut* (shamans) that the help of these spirits is essential. Without it, shamans cannot maintain their powers. From his adventures among the Eskimos of the Arctic Circle, Rasmussen observes: "It is not enough for a shaman to be able to escape both from himself and his surroundings. It is not enough that . . . he is able to withdraw the spirit from his body and thus undertake the great 'spirit flights' through space and through the sea. . . . For he will be incapable of maintaining these faculties unless he has the support of helping and answering spirits. . . . He cannot even choose for himself what sort he will have. They have to come to him of their own accord, strong and powerful."

Spirit helpers usually appear to the shaman during initiation. They enable the shaman to perform healings and other tasks in the spirit world. The spirits help diagnose the cause of an illness, recover a lost soul, or clear obstacles from the path to the spirit world.

Eskimos believe that the more helpers a shaman has, the more powerful the shaman is. The helping

Drawing of a shaman beating on her ceremonial drum.

spirits might be the souls of ancestors, plants, animals, or even spirits of the elements, such as wind or rain.

Shamans of North and South America, Siberia, and Australia usually have animal helpers. They are called "power animals." Shaman Rosie Plummer of the Paviotso people of Nevada inherited the rattlesnake as his helper: "Rattlesnake was my uncle's power; then my father had rattlesnake for his power. Now the snake gives me power. . . . The snake helps me doctor now. It comes to me when I dream."

Power animals are often bears, eagles, or owls. Among the Lapps, the reindeer is a common power animal. Wolves are common among shamans of Siberia and the Arctic. According to Joe Green of the Paviotso people, "One shaman may get his power from the hawk that lives in the mountains. Another may get his power from the eagle, the otter, or the bear. . . . When a shaman gets his power from the otter, it means that the spirit is from many otters. The chief otter spirit tells the man to be a good doctor. It is this main otter that cannot be seen by the common people. . . . Only the shaman can see him there."

Leaving Ordinary Reality

Shamans can become their power animal spiritually, taking on the special abilities and powers of the animal. During ceremonies, shamans may wear a mask or the skin and claws of the animal. Imitating the movements, growls, or calls of the power animal, the shaman "turns into" the animal. Shamans use sacred plants, dancing, and drumming to enter an altered state of consciousness. They may then travel to the spirit world in the form of the power animal.

Turning into a power animal is a way of leaving ordinary reality and connecting with the beyond. The change also stands for the deep connection between animals and humans. In many shamanic cul-

North American shaman dances in ceremonial elk headdress.

tures, it is believed that animals and humans were related when earth was a paradise. Joe Green says, "A long time ago, all the animals were Indians (they could talk). I think that is why the animals help the people to be shamans."

Spirit helpers are not unique to shamans. Many psychics claim to have spirits who speak through them. Some very famous people in history also claimed to have spirit helpers. The great psychologist Carl Jung said he had a spirit guide called Philemon. Philemon appeared during a very difficult period in Jung's life. The ancient Greek philosopher Socrates and the Indian leader Mahatma Gandhi also reported being guided by spirits.

Creations of the Imagination

Many mental health experts, however, doubt that the spirits actually exist. They say spirits are creations of the imagination. Spirit guides seem to appear in times of extreme stress, fatigue, hunger, thirst, or isolation. They say spirit helpers are like children's imaginary friends. The spirits give people someone to blame for their actions and decisions and to provide comfort when they are unhappy.

There is no clear-cut explanation for the source of the spirit guides, however. Jung believed Philemon was a being who came from deep within his unconscious. Philemon was an aspect of himself that had more wisdom. This aspect could speak honestly, without emotions getting involved. He said regardless of where spirit guides come from, they are of great therapeutic value.

Dr. Roger Walsh says that psychology may not know enough about the mind to figure out where spirit guides come from. In fact, they may not all come from the same place. He says, "For all we know, some might be merely aspects of mind . . . while others might . . . [come from] beyond us."

Some psychics and their spiritual guides suggest that the spirits come from within the mind and beyond at the same time. Psychic Eileen Garrett writes, "I asked these spirit figures if I was seeing them or if I was seeing what was in my own brain. They answered, 'Both.'" Seth was a famous spirit who spoke and wrote through a human named Jane Roberts. Seth also claimed to be both a separate entity and an extension of Roberts' consciousness.

Shamans would probably agree with Garrett's and Roberts' spirits. To the shaman, reality is not clear-cut. There are no real boundaries between the human mind and the universe.

Physics and the Shamans' Reality

In a world ruled by reason, nature follows certain rules. But in a world ruled by the supernatural, anything is possible. Animals talk. People fly. Time

Just as shamans claim to follow the directions of guiding spirits, so did renowned Swiss psychiatrist Carl Jung claim to listen to a guiding spirit named Philemon.

has no meaning. A shaman can dive into the earth and emerge into another world.

Most scientists dismiss the shamans' reality as fantasy—or insanity. But some modern physicists offer some intriguing ideas that someday might unlock the shamans' secrets.

An Interconnected Universe

As you have read, shamans believe all of the universe is interconnected. They believe that their super abilities come from being able to transcend (go beyond) the boundaries of time and space. They believe all things are part of the great fabric of the universe. And at the same time, each thing is a single thread in the fabric.

Physicist David Bohm's "holographic" concept of the universe is very similar. A hologram is a three-dimensional photograph made with lasers. If a hologram is cut into pieces and then a laser is shined through the pieces, each piece still contains an image of the entire picture. The image is blurry—but complete. That is, every piece contains information about the rest of the image as well as information about itself. Bohm suggests that the universe is a gigantic hologram. Every one of its parts, down to the smallest particle, contains a blurry version of the whole universe. This concept affects how we view reality. In a holographic universe, there is no time or three-dimensional space. Past, present, and future all exist at once. As in the shamanic view, in Bohm's holographic world there is no clear distinction between living and nonliving things either. For example, nonliving things, such as oxygen or carbon dioxide atoms, are needed for life to exist. So Bohm asks, can we really say oxygen and carbon dioxide are nonliving?

This holographic view of the universe also suggests awesome possibilities about the human mind. Each person has his or her own consciousness and separateness. But within that consciousness is also imprinted a blurry image or knowledge of the larger reality of the universe.

Perhaps that larger reality includes the spirit world or parallel worlds. And perhaps the shamans possess vast knowledge and power because they can see the holographic image more clearly than most other people can. This access to the entire image enables them to see distant places and even to travel there in an instant. They can see the future as if it is now. They see the spirit world as clearly as they see the physical world.

But how can the shaman—or the physicist—ever prove these versions of the universe and reality? The shaman sees no need for proof. "For the shaman, what one sees—that's real. . . . The shaman depends upon first-hand observation of what's real. If you can't trust what you see for yourself, then what can you trust?" says Michael Harner.

Modern physics may back up the shaman on that point! Physicists have discovered that observing subatomic particles actually changes their behavior. If this observation is applied to the physical world, then there can be no one objective reality. Objective reality is a reality that is absolute and unaffected by anyone or anything. However, we can never know if there is such a reality, because observing it changes it. We can never know what would have been if we had not observed it. So the only reality any of us can know is what each of us observes.

At first glance, the shamans' world may seem alien and fantastic to people in the modern scientific world. But upon closer inspection, the shamans' world and modern science may not be so far apart after all.

Three

How Does a Person Become a Shaman?

Most shamans are chosen or called by the spirits. The call may be a dramatic illness or accident or a change of behavior. The shamanic candidate may not listen to the call or recognize it as a call right away. But refusal to obey the call of the spirits can bring serious problems. Acceptance of the call finally leads to healing and initiation, which is a period of training.

The wife of Kyzlasov, a Sagay shaman in Siberia, told Hungarian explorer Vilmos Diószegi: "He who is seized by the shaman sickness and does not begin to exercise shamanism, must suffer badly. He might lose his mind, he may even have to give up his life. Therefore he is advised, 'You must take up shamanism so as not to suffer!' Some even say, 'I became a shaman only to escape illness.'"

The Call

Shamans may be "called spontaneously" by the spirits. Or they may inherit the position from ancestors or relatives. Some "choose themselves" by seeking and even paying for training. These shamans, however, are less powerful.

Spontaneous call. The spontaneous call from the spirits may take the form of physical or emotional illness. This usually happens in the teenage or

(opposite page) Alaskan Indian medicine man in ceremonial wolf costume.

Yenesei Ostyak, a shaman from northern Siberia, poses in traditional costume.

early adult years. The young person falls ill, has seizures or fits, or exhibits strange behavior. Shamanic candidates may become absentminded. They may spend a lot of time alone in their huts or wandering in the wilderness. They may begin to have strange dreams or sing in their sleep. A family or community member, the candidate, or a master shaman finally recognizes this behavior as a sign that the spirits have chosen the young person.

According to Mircea Eliade, future Yakut (Siberia) shamans become frenzied and withdraw to the forest. They eat tree bark, fling themselves into fire or water, and cut themselves with knives. They may flee to the mountains and eat animals that they catch with their teeth. They return to the village looking quite wild. Finally, they are taken in by the tribe's master shaman who teaches them about the spirits and how to contact them.

Visions in the Night

Many shamans learn through the dreams they have while ill that they must become shamans. Kyzlasov's wife told Diószegi: "Sickness seized him [Kyzlasov] when he was twenty-three years old and he became a shaman at the age of thirty. That was how he became a shaman, after the sickness, after the torture. . . . While he was ailing, he had dreams: He was beaten up several times, sometimes he was taken to strange places."

Among the Zulu, future shamans become ill and will only eat certain things. They complain of pain throughout their bodies and they dream a lot. They cry easily and loudly enough for the community to hear. They may remain ill like this for many years until they sing their first shamanic song. Dorcas, a Zulu shaman, was bedridden for three years before beginning her training. At night, though, she left her body and traveled far and wide. One night, her dead grandfather appeared in a dream. He said he would enter her body and continue his work as a shaman.

She was a devout Christian and resisted. But the spirit of her grandfather persisted. Her mother took her to a relative who was a shaman. She and other shamans beat their drums and called her to get up and sing. Finally Dorcas began to dance and sing. She continued for hours. She then began her training to become a shaman.

The shamans of the Kenyan Kikuyu are "called" by illness that includes strong dreams, visions, poor concentration, weakened eyesight, and bizarre behavior. The candidate's family may also endure accidents and other misfortunes. Another shaman must confirm, however, that this candidate is indeed being called to shamanize.

Sometimes, the call comes in the form of a serious and life-threatening accident. Among the Soyot of Siberia, a person who is struck by lightning becomes a shaman. An ordinary accident such as being bitten by a snake or falling from a tree can be a sign of selection, too. Among the Aymaras of Peru, a shaman must be struck twice by lightning—once to kill him and the other to revive him.

Candidates may also be called during a vision quest. This is a period of time a person spends alone and without food. A vision quest is undertaken in order to learn the purpose or direction for one's life. This is a common practice among Native Americans. If the person is to become a shaman, it is revealed in visions and dreams.

Chosen Shamans

Shamans who are called spontaneously are considered greater shamans than others because they are chosen by the spirits. The difficulties relating to their calls—the illnesses and strange behavior—are the result of their fighting the call of the spirits. Many men and women are at first reluctant to take on the great responsibility of being a shaman. When they accept the call and undergo the initiation the symptoms are relieved.

"The symptoms of this preliminary phase have led many investigators to suggest that in the tradition of shamanism primitive cultures have merely found a convenient way to accommodate their psychologically ill individuals. And there may indeed be a measure of truth in this."

Stephen Larsen, mythology expert

"The validity of both [physical and non-physical] realms is acknowledged by the shaman, whose mastery derives from his ability not to confuse the two."

Richard Noll, psychologist

Drawing depicting a shamanic initiation. The initiate within the cylinder-shaped hut learns the secrets of the animal spirits, shown descending upon the hut from the heavens.

Inherited calling. Shamans in cultures all over the world can inherit their office. Or they may be selected by the community, a shaman relative, or another master shaman. Aua, an Iglulik Eskimo, was selected even before birth. His parents had to follow strict diets and taboos before he was born and for many years after.

Even hereditary shamans are called or elected by the spirits though. Like those chosen spontaneously, they may show a change in behavior during their teenage years. They may even have a severe illness such as those described above.

Initiation

Shamanic candidates undergo an initiation period. This training can last anywhere from a few days to many years.

Some of the training is formal instruction. Master shamans and the spirits instruct them about healing, the names of the spirits and their functions, tribal lore, the geography of the spirit world, the natural world, and the use of sacred plants. The "student" shamans also learn how to interpret dreams, enter altered states of consciousness, and talk with the spirits.

Anthropologist Michael Harner says that the training consists of "learning successfully how to achieve the shamanic state of consciousness, and to see and journey in that state; acquiring . . . knowledge of one's guardian spirit . . . and learning successfully to help others as a shaman."

Physical Ordeal

Training to become a shaman often involves severe conditions. Those conditions may include extreme heat or cold, isolation, pain, monotony, days without sleep, food, or water, or use of sacred drugs. These extreme conditions are stressful to the body and mind. The stress induces ecstatic experiences, such as visions, dreams, and journeys. After initiation, the shamans rarely need these extreme measures to enter the shamanic state of consciousness. However, they may use some of them from time to time.

Caribou Eskimo shaman Igjugarjuk described his initiation. He told explorer Knud Rasmussen the initiation included starvation, cold, and isolation. In the middle of winter, his teacher took him to an isolated snow hut. The hut was only large enough for Igjugarjuk to sit in. After five days, his teacher brought him water. Fifteen days later, his teacher brought him more water. At the end of thirty days, his teacher brought him back to the village. Igjugarjuk was thin as a skeleton and nearly dead. But during his time in the cold, alone and hungry, he had kept his mind on the Great Spirit, he said. Toward the end of the thirty days, a spirit had come to him in the form of a woman. She became his helping spirit. For a year after this ordeal, the Eskimo shaman followed a special diet and other rules and finally became a shaman.

Igjugarjuk told Rasmussen: "The only true wisdom lives far from mankind, out in the great loneliness. It can be reached only through suffering. Privation and suffering alone can open the mind . . . to all that is hidden to others."

The Sweat Lodge

The extreme heat of a sweat lodge can also bring on an altered state. It is used not only by shamans, but as a cleansing and healing ritual by other people. The sweat lodge is a simple hut made of saplings and blankets. Red-hot rocks are placed in a fire pit in the center. The flap of the lodge is closed and water is poured over the stones to produce steam. Sioux shaman Leonard Crow Dog tells of his initiation at age twelve. Like Igjugarjuk, he endured severe conditions, including the heat of the sweat lodge and the fasting and isolation of the vision quest. "It was so hot," he said, "it came like a shock wave upon me. . . . I dared not breathe; I thought that if I did I would burn my lungs into charcoal. But I did not cry out. I just stuck my head between my knees."

He and his father and uncle and other relatives in the sweat lodge smoked a sacred pipe, then more stones were brought in. "The heat, the steam, the tobacco made me giddy and light-headed. It had emptied my mind so that the spirits could enter it. I felt weak, but I also felt power streaming through my veins, a new, strange power. As I stared into the flowing stones, I thought I saw a small bird in them."

After the sweat lodge, in which spirits appeared to all present and it seemed as if the very earth were moving, Crow Dog's uncle said the boy was purified and ready for his big dream or vision. He then was sent on a vision quest alone and without food for two days. He spent these two days at the end of a short tunnel under the ground. He had a great vision that revealed that he would indeed become a shaman.

Shamanic candidates also learn to put themselves into trances through monotony. Monotony is

Najagneg, an Eskimo shaman of Greenland.

the repeating of a sound or motion over and over again. Have you ever noticed that if you do the same action over and over again you "space out"? The student shamans of the Greenland Eskimos grind a small stone against a large rock for days. They do not even stop for food or water. One student said that on the second day, he saw a bear spirit rise from the lake. It grabbed him by the neck and dragged him into the water. He became unconscious. When he came to, he was on shore again and another spirit, a dwarf, was near him. As he started on his way home, completely naked, his clothing came flying to him. He still needed other helping spirits though, so he continued to rub the stone against the rock. Soon other spirits came to him to help him cure sick people.

The Yamana of Patagonia rub their cheeks for days on end. They are said to be rubbing through layers of consciousness to reach the shamanic state. Psychologist Holger Kalweit says, "It takes surprisingly little to turn human consciousness upside down. . . . Repeating an activity until one is exhausted is an important triggering mechanism for seeing spirits."

Body Control

Shamanic students train themselves to have complete control over their bodies. Some of them can even direct their body's processes to control their temperatures. According to researcher Jeanne Achterberg, shamans push the physical body to the limit. The "mind is unhinged from conventional reality." They use extreme conditions as a route to knowledge.

In many cultures shamanic training involves learning to use sacred plants. Sacred plants are used mostly in South and Central America where they grow naturally. The sacred plants bring on visions of the spirit world. They also intensify the senses and the experience of the physical world.

"There is no reason and no excuse for not considering the shaman as a severe neurotic and even as a psychotic."

George Devereaux, anthropologist

"We might consider that there are many natural shamans who are haunting the corridors of asylums, inmates who, under other circumstances, and with different training, could have been ecstatics and visionaries, evokers of the sacred in society, instead of maimed and miserable spirits."

Jean Houston, psychologist

According to anthropologist Neville Drury, the sacred plant is "a doorway to a realm that is awesome and wondrous, and the undertaking is not one which is taken lightly. . . . [It is taken] to 'learn' or to 'see,' not to escape into a world of 'fantasy'. . . . Sacred plants remove the barriers between humankind and the realm of gods and spirits." The sacred plants are often regarded as divine, as gods themselves, by the shamanic people. The sacred plant speaks through the shaman. Sacred plants may be used along with fasting, solitude, singing, and other rituals.

In Colombia, the Siona-Tukano spend a month in isolation so that their memory of the ordinary world will fade. During that time, they drink *ayahuasca*. This is a drink made from the bark of the banisteriopsis vine. With each training session, they acquire more shamanic knowledge.

Manuel Córdova-Rios is a shaman trained by the Amahuaca Indians of the Amazon jungle in South Ameria. He describes his training which included the use of an extract of *nixi honi xuma*, the very powerful *Banisteriopsis caapi* vine:

He was taken by the old shaman-chief to a small shelter just outside the village. After some preparation, the old shaman, chanting, handed him a gourd with the powerful drug. He instructed Córdova-Rios to "drink alone this time. I will be present to guide you." He explained that the younger man's strict diet and training before this had prepared him well. "Pleasant and profound visions will come to you."

Altered States

In a short time, Córdova-Rios became aware of "undreamed beauty in the details of the textures of leaves, stems, and branches. . . . Unimaginable detail of structure showed. . . . Time seemed suspended; there was only now and now was infinite. I could separate the individual notes of the bird song and savor each in its turn."

Córdova-Rios "could see things that in other circumstances would have been totally invisible" to him. When he "awoke," Córdova-Rios felt he was coming back "from a distant journey to unknown and unremembered places."

The training sessions continued—four sessions every eight days. He began to notice a change in his thought processes. "By focusing attention on a single individual I could divine his reactions and purposes and anticipate what he would do. . . . The old man said my power to anticipate and know future events would improve and grow."

Córdova-Rios says he believed the old shaman

Drawing depicting Eskimo spirits and chanting shaman.

was transmitting to him the tribal knowledge of centuries.

Death and rebirth are central to the initiation of a shaman. The candidate must undergo a death of the old self. A new self, which has great knowledge and understanding, is then born.

Death and rebirth usually occur in a big dream or vision. The dream may come while the person is unconscious from a serious illness or injury. Or it may take place during the formal training, brought on by the extreme conditions of initiation. The dream is a turning point. Candidates do not become shamans until they have this dream of death and rebirth.

A Rebirth

In many of these dreams and visions, the candidates are dismembered. That is, their bodies are taken apart. Or their organs or brains are removed and replaced. This all shows that the shamans have been cleansed and put together in a new way. The illusions, concerns, and evils of ordinary reality have been removed. The shamans are starting anew, with a new clearness of mind and understanding.

Here is a typical Siberian initiation vision, described in Mircea Eliade's book *Shamanism*:

Sick with smallpox, the shamanic candidate was unconscious for three days. He was so lifeless that his people had started making funeral plans. While his body lay "dead," though, his spirit was carried into the middle of the sea. His Sickness said to him, "From the Lords of the Water, you will receive the gift of shamanizing."

The Sickness moved the waters of the sea and the shaman emerged. He climbed a mountain and met the Lady of the Water and her husband, the Lord of the Underworld. He was given two guides, an ermine and a mouse, to lead him to the underworld. In the underworld, he met the lords of diseases and evil shamans. The guides led him to an island on which grew the Tree of the Lord of the Earth. The tree was surrounded by herbs, the ancestors of all the plants on earth. He was taught the healing abilities of the plants. The Lord of the Tree gave him a branch to make himself a shaman's drum.

The ermine and the mouse led him to many places where he learned how to shamanize and help people. Then the ermine and mouse led him to a distant mountain. When he entered a cave, he came upon a naked man working a bellows. The man cut off the shaman's head, chopped his body into pieces and put all the parts into a huge cauldron. The shaman's parts were boiled for three years. The man, a blacksmith, had three anvils. On the third one, the one on which the best shamans were forged, the smith forged a new head. Then he threw the head into a pot of cold water. This meant that the shaman's patients would heal only if the water in the ritual pot was very cold. Then the smith fished the shaman's bones out of the river and put them together again. He covered them with new flesh. He gave new eyes to the forged head. Now the shaman would see with these mystical eyes when he shamanized. The smith also pierced the shaman's ears so that he could understand the language of plants.

At last, the shaman awoke inside his yurt (tent). He was no longer sick. In fact, he was strong enough to shamanize for long periods without even growing tired.

Death by Dismemberment

Death by dismemberment, as described above, occurs often in initiation dreams. A bear devours Angmagsalik Eskimo shamans of Greenland during their initiation dream. The bear swallows shamans whole, then vomits them up bone by bone. Each shaman's bones are put back together and covered with new flesh.

"He [the bear] circled round me, bit me in the

"I had not been lying there long before I heard the bear coming. It attacked me and crunched me up, limb by limb, joint by joint, but strangely enough it did not hurt at all; it was only when it bit me in the heart that it did hurt frightfully. From that day forth I felt that I ruled my helping spirits. After that I acquired many fresh helping-spirits and no danger could any longer threaten me, as I was always protected."

Autdaruta, Greenland Eskimo shaman

"It is well known from many different sources that a limited supply of oxygen or an excess of carbon dioxide produces abnormal mental states. . . . Lack of oxygen can induce unusual experiences quite similar to LSD."

Stanislav Grof and Joan Halifax, medical researchers

loins, and then ate me. At first it hurt, but afterwards, feeling passed from me; but as long as my heart had not been eaten, I retained consciousness. But, when it bit me in the heart, I lost consciousness and was dead," says Sanimuinak, an Angmagsalik shaman of Greenland.

Far from Greenland and Siberia, among the Dyak of Borneo, the old shamans or spirits are said to remove the brain of the candidate. They wash it and return it with a clear mind. Among the Ungarinyin of northwest Australia, the skeleton spirits drag the candidate into the spirit realm where they take his or her brain out and replace it with a new one. Among western Australia's Warburton Ranges aborigines, spirits cut open the initiate's body. They remove the organs and replace them with magical substances. They also remove the shoulder bone and tibia, dry them, and stuff them with the same magical substances. In Dampier Land and the Lower Fitzroy River of Australia, the spirits cut open the candidate's body. They remove the organs and hang them up. They place the body over an earthen oven. Then they put the organs back. They place crystals in the navel and between the eyes and ears. They also give the new shaman an inner eye (or "strong eye") in order to see beyond time and space.

Similar accounts of torture, death, and rebirth at the hands of the spirits come from Africa and North and South America.

Enlightenment

Not until candidates have "died" and been cleansed and reborn can they become "enlightened." With enlightenment comes knowledge that was hidden before, knowledge of all things past, present, and future. An Eskimo shaman explained enlightenment to Rasmussen, the explorer: "Every real shaman has to feel an illumination in his body, in the inside of his head or in his brain, something

Diptych by fifteenth-century Dutch painter Hieronymus Bosch shows the entrance into paradise as a long tunnel leading to a brightly lighted world. Shamans report initiation experiences of death and rebirth similar to Bosch's depiction.

that gleams like fire, that gives him the power to see with closed eyes into the darkness, into the hidden things or into the future or into the secrets of another man. I felt that I was in possession of this marvelous ability."

Aua, an Eskimo shaman, describes his enlightenment: "I felt a great, inexplicable joy, a joy so powerful that I could not restrain it. . . . Then in the midst of such a fit of mysterious and overwhelming delight I became a shaman, not knowing myself how it came about. But I was a shaman. I could see and hear in a totally different way. I had gained my enlightenment, the shaman-light of brain and body, and this in such a manner that it was not only I who could see through the darkness of life, but the same light also shone out from me, imperceptible to human beings, but visible to all the spirits of earth and sky and sea, and these now came to me and became my helping spirits."

The Near-Death Experience and the Shaman

Is the dramatic initiation journey experienced by shamans really a near-death experience (NDE)? This is an experience in which a person almost dies or is clinically dead for a few minutes.

Researchers have interviewed thousands of people all over the world who have had near-death experiences. They include people who "died" during surgery or from heart attacks or accidents, as well as people who were very ill or unconscious. Many of them described a common experience.

They became aware of the consciousness, soul, or spirit leaving the body. The "spirit" was an energy field or something misty or cloudy that could travel through solid matter. They saw their physical bodies below them. Like shamans, most of these patients felt themselves being pulled into a long tunnel. At the end of the tunnel was a brilliant light, and they felt great peace and love. They also saw creatures of light, spirits of friends and relatives who had died at an earlier time, and even spirit helpers. These spirits communicated with the patients through the mind. The patients also saw a lightning-fast review of their entire lives.

Then they entered a world of brilliant colors and light. Their senses were heightened. Time had no meaning—present, past, and future all existed at once. Many people reported that they felt as if they had gained total knowledge, or enlightenment—they could understand the mysteries of the universe.

Most people who have a near-death experience are changed by it. They experience a "rebirth." They become more interested in spirituality and in serving their communities. Shamans are "reborn" after their initiation journeys, too. They learn special powers of healing, and they begin to serve their communities. Unlike people who have had NDEs, however, shamans can return to the other world whenever they choose.

Scientists are seeking explanations for near-death visions. Many researchers say the near-death experience is caused by *anoxia*. That is a delirium brought about by lack of oxygen. Some say that during this delirium, patients use fantasy to try to deal with their fears about dying.

Other reseachers suggest that the brain may release a natural narcotic that brings about an out-of-body experience similar to that experienced while using hallucinogenic drugs. Medical researchers Stanislav Grof and Joan Halifax used LSD therapy to help cancer patients deal with their coming deaths. LSD is a hallucinogenic drug. Many of these patients underwent journeys similar to those of the shamanic initiation. They experienced "hell" as well as "paradise."

Medical researchers do not agree on the specific reactions that trigger the near-death experiences. But they do believe that the process of dying triggers biological, chemical, and electrical reactions. Those reactions most likely account for the dying or "dead" person's experiences. Those physical reactions might also account for the shamans' initiation experience, say some researchers.

Without question, the shamanic vision experience is closely tied to death. Don Eduardo Calderon, a Peruvian shaman, states that learning to die is one of the most important lessons for a shaman's apprentice. Shamans are considered masters of death. Once they have confronted their own death, they will no longer be afraid of anything.

Is Initiation a Call to Mental Illness?

To many mental health experts, the shaman's initiation visions are not mystical; they are symptoms of mental illness. The initiation vision is part

Drawing of Don Eduardo Calderon, a Peruvian shaman, performing a ritual using a Spanish saber and Christian cross.

of an ongoing illness, say these experts. If the "patients" are not treated, they stay in a world of fantasy. The bizarre behaviors, visions, and talks with spirits all show that the shamans are out of touch with reality.

Anthropologist Åke Ohlmarks studied shamanism among Arctic tribes in the 1930s. He believed that the shamans' trances were caused by "Arctic hysteria." The severe conditions—cold, long nights, isolation, and hunger—led to mental illness. But since shamanism is found in many different climates, Ohlmarks' theory has been rejected by most anthropologists.

Psychiatrist Julian Silverman, however, agrees with Ohlmarks that shamans are mentally ill. He writes that the shaman is definitely schizophrenic. He says that the shaman shares many symptoms with schizophrenic people: strange behavior, intense emotional fits, and the inability to tell the difference between reality and fantasy. Schizophrenic people withdraw from others. They also claim that other beings or people have put thoughts in their minds or are speaking through them.

There is only one major difference between schizophrenic people and shamans, Silverman says. That difference is in how their communities treat them. Schizophrenic people are labeled mentally ill and treated as if they are sick. Their experiences are dismissed as fantasy. But shamans are accepted by their communities. They are even encouraged to practice their fantasies. At the first signs of madness—shamans are *trained* into further madness.

Initiation as a Cure

Other experts take the view that shamans are sick people who have been healed. Through the initiation and the support of the community, they learn to handle their "problems." The initiation is a "rebuilding process." The shamans learn to understand their "inner journey" and how it fits into their lives. Psychiatrist John Perry says that if society tells schizophrenic people they are crazy, then they soon think they are crazy. But if "sick" people are supported and not made to feel crazy, they may come through the process "enriched" and even healed. When shamans try to fight off the call of the spirits and stay "sane," the symptoms get worse. But once the shaman accepts the spirits, the symptoms lessen. And after the initiation, they are able to control the spirits—and the madness.

That control is the major difference between shamans and people with schizophrenia, agrees psychologist Richard Noll. People with schizophrenia have no control over the visions, voices, and spirits. They are bombarded. Shamans, however, learn to

66

"The shaman is not only a sick man; he is, above all, a sick man who has been cured, who has succeeded in curing himself."

Mircea Eliade, religion scholar

"We cannot treat all shamans as simply self-healed neurotics or psychotics."

I.M. Lewis

master ordinary and nonordinary reality. They are well aware of what they are doing and where they are.

Still other mental health experts say it is offensive to apply the label of "insanity" to shamans. Most shamans are healthy, respected members of their communities. Calling them insane is "ethnocentric" thinking. Ethnocentric means looking at other cultures and judging them according to one's own culture's values and customs. In an ethnocentric view, non-Christian, non-"modern" cultures are usually considered backward. The beliefs of people in these cultures are dismissed as "primitive," backwards, and false. Ethnocentric beliefs lead to prejudice. People start to believe that anything that is different is invalid, or "weird,"—or a form of insanity. Jeanne Achterberg says the view that the shaman is mentally ill stems from an ethnocentric belief: Any behavior is crazy if it is not within the modern world's idea of normal.

Psychiatrists such as R.D. Laing and Thomas Szasz also talk about the ethnocentric definition of madness. They say madness is "in the eye of the beholder." That is, a person's own culture defines sanity and insanity. Shamans may be considered insane if judged by our values and behavior. But, they wonder, why should our society's standards be the standards for the rest of the world? The shamans' communities accept the shaman's behavior. In fact, *not* believing in spirits would be insane to shamanic people.

Is the Initiation Experience "Real"?

What is the true nature of this initiation experience? It may be a product of the imagination. It may have a physical or biological basis, as experts on death and dying suggest. Or it may actually be a spiritual experience.

The explanations of "experts" do not matter to the shaman. According to Michael Harner, shamans would not care if science could prove these experiences were all in the shaman's mind. That would not make the spirit realm any less real to him or her.

For shamans, experience is proof enough that the initiation journey was real. Throughout their lives, they continue to prove their experiences are real by returning, at will, to the other world. The initiation journey happened as it happened. Eskimo shaman Najagneg sums it up: "I have searched in the darkness, being silent in the great lonely stillness of the dark. So I became an *angakok* [shaman], through visions and dreams and encounters with flying spirits."

Four

What Are the Shaman's Tools?

During initiation, shamans learn to leave ordinary reality and to journey in soul form to other worlds. The journey, or soul flight, is at the heart of shamanism. It is the activity that makes a shaman a shaman. Once initiated, shamans make the journey again and again, but now they make the journey by choice.

To help them alter their consciousness and journey—and then find their way back—shamans use a number of tools and techniques. Their methods are remarkably similar around the world.

Throughout the world, percussion instruments, especially drums, are a vital part of the shaman's equipment. The instrument makes contact with the spirit world.

The drum may be decorated with drawings. It usually has feathers, fur, or bells hanging from it. Some shamans decorate the drum with horse symbols. To the shaman the drum is like a horse or other animal to "ride" into the spirit world. In the song below, Siberia's Soyot shamans ask the drum to "carry" them:

Skin-covered drum,
Fulfill my wishes,
Like flitting clouds, carry me
Through the lands of dusk

(opposite page) Nineteenth-century woodcut of Tlingit Eskimo shaman chanting over sick man while the man's family watches and prays.

And below the leaden sky,
Sweep along like wind
Over the mountain peaks!
Soyot shaman's song

The drum also has a link with the initiation journey. In some tribes, shamanic candidates visit the World Tree. The spirits instruct the candidates to make a drum from a branch of the tree. When back in ordinary reality, each new shaman finds a tree that represents the World Tree. The shaman cuts and hollows a piece of the tree and stretches an animal skin over the top. Because the drum is made from the sacred World Tree, when shamans beat their drums, they easily return to the center of the universe, the World Axis.

Among Australia's shamanic people, it is the echo of the drumming that is important. They say the sound travels around the mountaintops. The sound brings the spirits living there to the physical world. It also helps the shaman enter the trance state.

Scientists have studied the shaman's use of the drum to enter an altered state of consciousness. They report that the steady pounding of the drum produces changes in the central nervous system. The low frequency of the drumbeats transmits energy to the brain. The shaman's drumbeat is very regular, at a specific number of beats per second. The steady sound allows the shamans to shut out distractions. It helps them relax and enter the shamanic state. Shamans have learned to associate the drum with the altered state. After only a few minutes of drumming, they can "ride" into the other world.

Shamans or their helpers also shake rattles to keep time and to "dance the spirits." According to Michael Harner the rattles reinforce the drumbeat. Many rattles are made from dried gourds filled with pebbles or seeds, then attached to a handle. In South

America, quartz crystals are put in the rattle. (The crystals are the shaman's spirit helpers. They will help the shaman heal patients.) Rattles made of hoof, bone, or tanned hide are also worn as anklets and bracelets. Shamans wear these when dancing. Some Siberian costumes are decorated with thirty to fifty pounds of metal ornaments. They rattle when the shaman dances.

Australian shamans use "click sticks" which are cylindrical pieces of hard wood strung together. They make a sharp, rapping sound.

The Shaman's Song

Song is another powerful instrument. The shaman uses the energy of song as a sacred tool to travel to nonordinary reality. Anthropologist Neville Drury

South African tribesmen use skin-covered drums during ceremony.

Hand-held ceremonial drum in the form of a crocodile. Animal skin covers one end to make the drumhead.

explains, "songs are the sounds of the gods and spirits and, like the sacred drum, can help the shaman feel propelled by their energy."

Apache shaman and chief Geronimo said, "As I sing, I go through the air to a holy place where Yusun [Supreme Being] will give me power to do wonderful things. I am surrounded by little clouds, and as I go through the air I change, becoming spirit only."

Among the Klamath people, the word meaning *spirit* also means *song*. Eskimo shaman Orpingalik says, "It is just as necessary for me to sing as it is to breathe."

Some shaman songs are handed down from generation to generation. Australian shamans sing many songs they believe their ancestors sang in the Dreamtime—the other world. So the songs are a link with the ancestors and with the Dreamtime.

Shamans also create their own songs, which they believe spring from their contact with the divine. North American Gitksan shaman Isaac Tens tells of the song that came from deep within his heart. At age thirty, he began seeing visions, and on his return from a hunting trip, he fell into a trance: "While I remained in this state, I began to sing. A chant was coming out of me without my being able to do anything to stop it. Many things appeared to me presently: huge birds and other animals. They were calling me. . . . These were visible only to me, not to the others in my house. Such visions happen when a man is about to become a halaait [shaman]; they occur of their own accord. The songs force themselves out, complete, without any attempt to compose them."

Shamans often chant power songs to put them in an altered state. They may sing the same song twenty or thirty times. Like the drum, the monotonous song gives the shamans something to focus on and to "carry them away." The songs get faster as the shamans approach the other world. Michael Harner suggests that the steady breathing during the singing helps the shamans alter their consciousness. This works in the same way steady breathing helps people relax or meditate.

During a ritual, the audience also might chant to

Drawing of Indian men and women chanting around a ceremonial fire. Visions in the flames and smoke often appeared to the entranced participants.

help the shaman reach the other world. The audience becomes relaxed. Their consciousness is altered too. They become more open to the world of the spirits. After some time, the shaman stops singing and only the audience sings. The shaman prepares to meet the spirits. When the spirits are in contact, the shaman signals the audience to stop singing.

Orpingalik says, "Songs are thoughts, sung out with the breath when people are moved by great forces and ordinary speech no longer suffices. . . . It will happen that the words we need will come of themselves. When the words we want to use shoot up of themselves—we get a new song."

Psychologists talk about ego. Shamans talk

Participants in a Tibetan ceremony wear skeleton costumes to depict the spirits of the dead.

about heart. But both agree that the songs come about when shamans forget their own significance and see that they are simply part of the universe. The song or chant is an expression of the power and beauty of the universe. The shaman is one small part of this great universe, along with the wind, the rains, the birds, the smallest insects, the grass, and the trees. Aua, an Eskimo shaman, describes how a song came to him: "Then, for no reason . . . I felt a great, inexplicable joy, a joy so powerful that I could not restrain it, but had to break into song, a mighty song, with only room for the one word: joy, joy! And I had to use the full strength of my voice."

Does song really have great power? Psychologist Holger Kalweit says that sound can have a profound physical and psychological effect on animals, including humans. He says that the Japanese samurai can "paralyze his opponent" with a scream of the right pitch. Among some Eastern philosophies, sound and vibration are believed to have healing and even supernatural powers. If sound is so powerful, then perhaps the pitch and vibration of the shaman's song can heal. Think about how different kinds of music affect people's emotions, and emotions have a big impact on health!

Costume

In most parts of the world, the shaman's costume is an important part of his or her practice. Costumes of the Siberian shamans are among the most ornate. Australian shamans, on the other hand, wear only a few body paintings.

The act of putting on the costume is a preparation and signal that the shaman will "travel" to the other world. The costume is filled with power because the spirits inhabit it. No one may wear the costume who cannot control the spirits.

The costumes often look like the animals that are special to the tribe or the shaman. Shamans wear bear, wolf, eagle, owl, otter, reindeer, or other

"The resemblance to stage illusion is striking."

Anthropologist Weston LaBarre

"One can only conclude that the world of the shaman, bizarre as it must sometimes seem to outsiders, is nevertheless totally real to the person experiencing it."

Anthropologist Neville Drury

animal costumes. Commonly, the costumes are decorated with animal pelts, claws, and feathers as well as ribbons and metal ornaments. A shaman's costume may also have embroidered rainbows, trees, stars, moon, sun, or other symbols. Each item of the costume means something to the shamans. It may stand for helping spirits, the upper or lower worlds, the World Axis, magical flight, healing, death, and rebirth.

The costumes and ornaments help the shaman pass between the worlds. Feathers, especially from cagles and owls, are common decoration all over the world. The shamans believe the feathers aid them on their magical flights.

Shamans in Japan wear capes decorated with stuffed snakes. Some Siberian shamans wear long ribbons or pelts that stand for snakes. Snakes, like horses, help the shaman journey to the other world.

Some costumes feature iron decorations that look like bones. Or the entire costume may look like a skeleton. The skeleton or bone decorations proclaim that the shaman is a master of the realm of death. The shaman can journey to the land of the dead and return. It also stands for the shaman's own death and rebirth during initiation.

The headpiece has great supernatural power. Among some groups, it is the most important part of the costume. The Siberian shaman's cap has dead lizards or other animals, feathers, and ribbons hanging from it. The cap also may have iron horns representing the reindeer or other horned animal. Siberia's Teleut shamans' caps are made from the body of the brown owl, including the wings and head. Japanese shamans wear caps with eagle and owl feathers.

Dance

Through dance, shamans are said to transform into their power animal. Wearing the animal costume, the shaman dances and makes noises like an animal. The repetitive movements—and exhaustion—can bring about an altered state of consciousness. A shaman of the Pacific Northwest says, "When I dance, I don't act, just follow your power, just follow the way of your power."

To the shaman and the audience, the shaman becomes the animal. The outward dance and costume reflect what is happening in the spirit world. The shaman's soul transforms into an animal. The shaman becomes the bear or the otter or the eagle. The shaman assumes the powers of the animal being danced.

Shamanic people also believe that humans were once much more powerful than they are today. Long, long ago, humans could physically change themselves into animals. The shamans' dance helps to recall and relive that powerful time.

African shaman, or witch doctor, wearing animal-skin headdress and necklace of magical herbs and carved objects.

Some anthropologists tend to view these "transformations" as trickery. The audience has been hypnotized or sent into a trance state through singing, drumming, and dancing. They are ready to believe anything. The costume, movements, and animal calls all deceive the audience into believing that the shaman really has become the animal. But Harner says that there is no attempt to trick anyone. The shaman and the community are dealing with another reality. The modern world's rules of logic do not apply. The shaman *is* the animal because the shaman has become the animal on a spirit level.

Medicine Bundle

Like other medicine men and women, the shaman has a sacred medicine bundle. In the bundle are "power objects" used for healing. The bundle may include crystals, pebbles, dried plants, bones, feathers, and so on. These are objects that the shaman associates with power places or important events.

Quartz crystals are important in many places around the world. For thousands of years, shamans in North and South America, Australia, and Southeast Asia have considered crystals as spirit helpers. Crystals are seen as solidified light from the sky or fragments from the heavens. Shamans use crystals for diagnosis and healing of disease. The crystals give them spirit vision (the "strong eye").

The bundle is opened during healing ceremonies. The shaman uses the power objects in the bundle to tap the healing energy of the spirits.

Drugs

Sacred drugs are used by shamanic people throughout the world but especially in Mexico and South America. They are never used just for fun. Central America's Mazatec shaman María Sabina says, "One has to show respect for the mushrooms. I felt within myself that they were related to me. They were like my parents, they were my blood."

Sacred drugs produce visions of things that do not exist in the physical world. The shamans use the plants to alter consciousness and gain access to the spirit world. The drugs bring on a wide range of visions, from swirling or geometric patterns, to intense colors and sounds, to journeys to the beginning of time.

In South America, shamans use a drink called *ayahuasca* or *yaje* or *caapi*. It is brewed from the banisteriopsis vine. Anthropologist and shaman Michael Harner says that *ayahuasca* produces a feeling that the soul is separate from the body and is able to travel. Users also see visions of animals and distant cities and people. They also feel that they are in contact with the supernatural.

South American shaman Manuel Córdova-Rios describes using an extract of the vine. Time lost all meaning. He could communicate telepathically with the shaman training him. He felt as if he and the shaman were one person. His senses became very acute. He could summon a vision of any creature and see its finest details. "My visual perception

Quartz crystals are often used by shamans as spirit helpers from the mineral world.

This mushroom contains a hallucinogenic chemical that causes expanded awareness and visions. It is used by Indian medicine people for religious purposes.

seemed unlimited. Never had I perceived visual images in such detail before. . . . A passing firefly lit up the scene with a brilliance that seemed to approach the light of day. My sense of hearing was also much more acute. I could separate the night sounds far and near."

Psilocybe mushrooms are commonly used by shamans in Mexico. These sacred mushrooms are used for diagnosis of illness. The users' senses of hearing, sight, and touch may be intensified. But Mazatec shaman María Sabina warns that not everybody who takes it "enters into the world where everything is known." She calls the sacred mushroom the *teo-nanácatl,* which means "divine flesh." "The mushroom is similar to your soul. It takes you where the soul wants to go," says Sabina.

She took the mushrooms to help her heal her people. The first time, the mushrooms told her what herbs her sick uncle needed and where they grew.

"The mushroom is similar to your soul. It takes you where the soul wants to go."

Shaman María Sabina

"A pill . . . is not a spiritual labor-saving device, salvation, instant wisdom."

Sidney Cohen, medical doctor

North American Indian shamans in Mexico and the southwest United States believe the peyote cactus contains a mind-expanding chemical that induces religious experiences.

She picked the herbs and prepared them. Her uncle got better. The mushrooms also brought her deep knowledge of the workings of the universe. During a mushroom journey, a spirit showed her a book and although she could not read, she was reading it. "In that one moment I learned millions of things. I learned and learned," she says. She "saw close by, the sun and moon because the more you go inside the world of *teo-nanácatl,* the more things are seen. And you also see our past and our future, which are there together as a single thing already achieved, already happened." She even saw the death of her own son and the knife that would kill him.

Peyote cactus is also found in Mexico. It produces a wide range of effects: vivid images, auras around objects, feelings of weightlessness, and heightened senses. There may also be overwhelming feelings of euphoria (joy) and a sense of being one with the universe.

San Pedro is a cactus and one of the most ancient of sacred plants in South America. It is made into a drink. When it is consumed, it produces drowsiness, then great insight, and finally a feeling of traveling across time and space.

Tobacco, alone or with another plant, is used by shamans in some parts of South America. The tobacco may be smoked or made into a drink. Among native peoples, tobacco is often offered to the gods as a sign of respect and appreciation.

Shamans warn that the sacred drugs must be taken with proper training and during a ritual. Otherwise, use of the drug is meaningless and even dangerous. The mind must be prepared for the visions produced by the drugs. The distractions of this world must be cleared away. If the mind is not prepared, the images can be overwhelming and very frightening.

How Sacred Drugs Work

Scientists suggest two different ways that these drugs bring visions. One is by expanding the shaman's internal perceptions. That is, the visions already exist in the minds of the users. The drugs arouse the imagination or release deeply buried memories. Some scientists even believe the drugs may allow the user to tap into the "collective unconscious." This is a concept proposed by psychologist Carl Jung. The collective unconscious is a set of memories held by all people and buried deep within the unconscious mind.

The second way sacred drugs may work is by expanding external perceptions to let in a larger view of reality. Scientists explain that brain chemistry is very delicately balanced. Any change can greatly alter perceptions. Normally, the brain releases a substance called *serotonin*. Serotonin screens out too much stimulation. It acts as a filter for perceptions. When drugs, or extreme conditions, stop the release of serotonin, perceptions are opened to a larger view of the world. For example, imagine that you suddenly have microscopic vision. The world of tiny organisms suddenly becomes visible.

That reality was always there, but you could not see it because it was too small. Scientists suggest that somehow the drugs remove the brain's filter and a more vivid view of reality comes pouring in.

Séance

The séance is the central public ceremony for the shaman. It is an important ceremony for healing, the conducting of souls to the lower world, and guidance. Shaman and audience take part through drumming, singing, dancing, or even taking a sacred drug. The audience is likely to be in an altered state, too.

Investigator Wilhelm Radlov tells of a séance he witnessed in Siberia in the late 1800s. It was held to conduct the soul of a dead woman to the lower world. The séance took place in the evening. The shaman circled the yurt and beat his drum. Then he entered the yurt and called the dead woman. His voice changed and he spoke in a high voice—the voice of the woman. Through the shaman, she complained that she did not know the way to the spirit world and was afraid to leave her family. She agreed, however, to let the shaman lead her to the lower world. They set off together on the journey. The shaman bargained with the souls of the lower world to accept the woman. The second part of the séance chronicled his journey back to physical reality. During his return, he danced and shouted until he collapsed.

Joel, a young man from New York, describes a séance conducted by Adamie, a Dogrib shaman of Canada: "Suddenly the drumming seemed louder and louder. The pitch became unbearable. It screamed like thunder over a lake." Joel says that Adamie leaped up amidst great animal cries. A metal ornament the shaman wore rang "like a thousand bells gone berserk." Joel felt great "turmoil." He saw birds flying through the room. A force pulled him into the dance. He lost track of time.

Some experts think séances are simply theatrics. Shamans know how to trick observers into believing in the shaman's supernatural powers. In the early 1900s, explorer Waldemar Bogoras described Siberia's Chukchee shamans as masters of ventriloquism and sleight of hand. He said the shamans are tricksters, although talented ones!

The Séance as Theater

Bogoras tells of a séance in a small, darkened room. The shaman beats his drum and sings, his voice becoming louder and louder. Within the small room, his voice echoes in all directions. He changes his voice by singing into the drum while beating it. Soon, the audience can no longer locate the source of the sounds.

After fifteen to thirty minutes of singing, the shaman begins to beat his drum faster and more violently. He is signaling that a spirit has entered his body. The shaman shouts wildly. Shaking his head, his teeth chatter loudly. He shrieks in a strange voice.

Voices seem to come from near and far away. Some voices seem to rush through the room, others to come from under the ground. The shaman plays tricks with the sounds of birds and animals and even the howling wind. "The walrus and the bear roar, the reindeer snorts, the wolf howls, the fox bays, the raven caws," Bogoras reports. The animal spirits are also able to talk.

"Tricks of various kinds break up the monotony of the performance," Bogoras observes. The spirits seem to scratch on the walls or run in all directions with their feet clattering. Wood, stones, cold water, or lumps of snow are tossed around. Sometimes the entire tent seems to shake. Bogoras suggests that the shaman's assistants help accomplish these "tricks."

Once the spirits are present and have everyone's attention, the shaman proceeds to the reason for the séance. He relays instructions or predictions from

"The shaman is not conscious of acting a part: he becomes in his own mind the animal. . . . To the audience, too, this strange figure, with its wild, frenzied appearance, its ventriloquistic cries, and its unearthly falsetto gabble . . . is no longer a human being but the thing it personifies. Their minds become receptive to the wildest imaginings and they see the strangest and most fantastic happenings."

Anthropologist Diamond Jenness

"The feeling of being in direct contact with the Truth is no guarantee that such contact has actually been achieved. . . . A primary rule of science is that you must test your understandings against the observable area of reality/experience to which they apply."

Psychologist Charles Tate

the spirits to various members of the audience.

According to Bogoras, the songs and drumming help hypnotize the audience. The ceremonies take place in the dark, too. All of these factors help make the supernatural "performance" convincing. He also writes that even if there are many spirit voices in the small room, they only speak one at a time. This seems to be proof to Bogoras that the shaman is creating the spirit voices by "throwing his voice."

Bogoras adds that the shamans do not even journey to the spirit world, even though their folklore is full of such adventures. A shaman may "pretend" to journey, but only for the wealthiest patients. And when he "returns" from the spirit world, he recites only memorized chants about how to heal the illness.

Suspicious Techniques

Even some shamans are suspicious of each other's theatrical techniques. Eskimo shaman Igjugarjuk was present at the séances of a coastal Eskimo shaman. He told Knud Rasmussen: "These angakut [shamans] never seemed trustworthy to me. It always appeared to me that these salt-water angakut attached more weight to tricks that would astonish the audience, when they jumped about the floor and lisped all sorts of absurdities and lies in their so-called spirit language; to me all this seemed only amusing and as something that would impress the ignorant. A real shaman does not jump about the floor and do tricks, nor does he seek by the aid of darkness, by putting out the lamps, to make his neighbors uneasy. For myself, I do not think I know much, but I do not think that wisdom or knowledge about things that are hidden can be sought in that manner."

Even though Igjugarjuk said these shamans are too theatrical, he did not dispute their great power. He warned that they can still "kill through words and thoughts." Shamans are so powerful that by concentrating on a person, they can send healing or illness and even death.

Séances may include some "staged events." But most shamanic séances are sincerely undertaken to help people, not trick them. The shamans' methods break down the boundaries between ordinary and nonordinary reality. They allow people to experience some part of the shamans' reality. The séance reminds them that the spirits exist and have great power.

The shamans' work may seem strange. Some of the methods may seem like tricks. It would be easy to dismiss the shamanic séance as good theater, and nothing more—if it were not for the fact that the séance often produces very real healing.

Photograph of Igjugarjuk, a powerful Eskimo shaman and chief wearing the garb of Danish Greenlanders. He would not allow his photo to be taken in his native caribou-skin outfit.

Five

How Do Shamans Heal?

(opposite page) Drawing of an Indian medicine man chanting and using a gourd rattle while performing a healing ritual.

Shamans are healers. They say they work with the spirits to heal people. Willidjungo, a Murngin shaman in Australia, says, "When I treat people those two [helping spirits] go right inside a man."

Healing ceremonies may be very ornate, with costumes and several days of rituals in which the entire community takes part. Or they can be very simple. Australian shaman Mun-yir-yir tells of such a healing: "Some of the people said to me, 'We are sick here in the chest. . . . Please Mun-yir-yir, help us.' I went then and took a shell and filled it with water and washed my hands. I felt over their chests and took out a bone and showed them. A man came from another country. He had a sore back. He said, 'I can't walk.' I looked from a long way and I saw that little hard thing inside him. I blew on his back and this thing came out a long way. . . . His back didn't hurt him and he was very pleased."

Some scientists and anthropologists claim that shamans' ceremonies are filled with trickery. They say the shamans' work does not have any real physical effect on the patient. Any improvements are temporary. Or the patient's problem was emotional or mental to begin with.

Other mental health and medical experts admire

the shamans. They say shamans are talented counselors who have mastered the use of suggestion, hypnosis and imagination in healing. But even these admirers think the shaman is working with the mind, not the spirits.

Shamans and their communities, however, do not look for any medical explanation for the healing work. They believe shamans are masters of the sacred realm, travelers in the spirit world. They are doing just what they claim. They are healing the patient.

These differing opinions spring from very different views about the structure of the world and about health.

What Is Health?

In the modern world, most medical doctors consider health to be a physical condition. Disease is explained as distress to an organ or body system. The distress is caused by infection, virus, or another microscopic culprit.

Shamans, on the other hand, believe physical health depends upon spiritual health. Health requires that a person walk in balance with nature, oneself, other people, and the spirits. An illness or

A South American shaman using magic in an attempt to draw an illness out of his patient's body.

injury is a gift. It reveals that there is a spiritual or emotional imbalance that must be healed.

Jeanne Achterberg, a medical researcher, offers this description of the shamanic view of health in her book *Imagery in Healing: Shamanism and Modern Medicine*: "Health is being in harmony with the world view. Health is an intuitive perception of the universe and all its inhabitants as being one fabric. Health is maintaining communication with the animals and plants and minerals and stars. . . . Health is expanding beyond one's singular state of consciousness to experience the ripples and waves of the universe."

To the shaman, maintaining power and balance is essential to health. By power, the shaman means *personal* power, the abundant energy, will, and ability that are available to all people. The spirit "provides a *power-full* body that resists the intrusion of external forces. . . . There is simply not room in a power-filled body for the easy entrance of . . . harmful energies known in ordinary reality as diseases," Michael Harner explains. "Being *power-full* is like having a force field in and around you."

While the goal of most medical doctors is to prolong life, the shamans' goal is to restore spiritual balance by restoring the patient's power. The medical doctor treats the illness; the shaman believes power must be restored before the illness can be treated.

The Causes of Illness

The medical doctor seeks the cause of an illness in the cells, tissues, organs, immune system, or other body system. The shaman looks for supernatural reasons: Why are the gods angry? Did an enemy use evil magic against the patient?

The gods may send disease because a person broke a taboo about sex, food, or hunting. They may send disease because the patient failed to honor the gods, broke a vow, stole, or even fought

"There are probably not
many modern physicians in
our culture who would
approve of shamanic
techniques as part of a
patient's course of
treatment."

Religion expert Gary Doore

"In traditional tribal medicine
and in Western practice from
its beginning in the work of
Hippocrates, the need to
operate through the patient's
mind has always been
recognized."

Physician Bernie Siegel

with a spouse. Unanswered dreams are another major cause of illness. The dreamer or a relative may fall ill if he or she does not obey instructions given by the spirits in a dream.

The Achomawi people of North America divide the causes of illnesses into six broad groups: accidents; breach of taboo; terror caused by seeing monsters; "bad blood"; poisoning by a shaman; and loss of the soul. Other communities may have other categories for illness. But in all shamanic communities, soul loss is the basic and most important cause of sickness.

Soul Loss or Scientific Medicine?

Soul loss leads to serious illness and even to death if the soul is not returned. The soul might escape during sleep, a yawn, a sneeze, or an accident. During sleep the soul might wander off and be captured by an enemy or have an accident that prevents its return. According to Harner, the Jívaro of South America believe the soul resides in the blood and may escape if a person bleeds. Shock or fright can also drive the soul away. Greenland Eskimos believe each part of the body has a soul. A problem in a part of the body is caused by its soul's departure.

Some tribes believe loss of one's power animal can cause illness. Such a loss leaves a person in a weakened condition. Then the patient is vulnerable to object or spirit intrusion: A spirit, enemy shaman, or magician can cause an object or an evil spirit to enter the weakened person's body. In order to cure the patient, the shaman must remove the intruder. The shaman may remove a small animal, a lizard, a stone, a crystal, a spider, a thorn, a piece of grain, or a piece of plant, for example. The *object* is not the cause of the illness; it is a *symbol* of the intruding spirit. The intruder interferes with the normal functioning of the body.

Most physicians dismiss the shamanic view of disease. They worry that shamans do more harm than good when their people rely on shamanic "superstition." Physicians point to the improved health of shamanic people since modern medicine was introduced.

Shamans do not deny that medical science is helpful and effective. They say that medical science and shamanism can be partners. Shamanism always has existed alongside other healing traditions—use of herbs or body work (massaging or other manipulation), for example. The shamans claim that their healings restore power. If the patient is stronger, medical treatment will work better.

For the shaman, the scientific and shamanic views of disease can both be true. Shamanism and science can exist side-by-side in a balance because health is balance. The shamans say that even if an illness can be traced to science's microorganisms, it might still be caused by the supernatural. A spirit or magician could have sent the organism. After all, they ask, why did that particular person get sick?

Some medical experts are beginning to see that the shamanic and scientific explanations of illness are not so different. The shaman speaks of loss of spirit, and this loss of spirit leaves a person open to object or spirit intrusion. Physicians now know that depression and anxiety can wear down defenses and leave the body weak—loss of spirit! Microorganisms are able to storm the weakened person and take hold in their bodies—object intrusion!

Diagnosis

In many cultures all over the world, shamans use divination to diagnose illness. Divination is discovering hidden information through supernatural methods. It is done in many different ways. Siberia's Samoyed shamans throw a marked stick into the air. The position of the stick when it lands tells the shaman about the illness. Shamans in Melanesia in the South Pacific gaze into a quartz crystal or a bowl of water. Some Eskimo shamans

An African shaman in a leopard-skin shirt reads a tribeswoman's future using various ritual objects, including a dried octopus and lizardskin.

use a head-lifting test. They hold the patient's head and ask questions regarding the source of the illness. If the weight of the head stays the same or becomes lighter, the answer is no. If the head becomes heavy, the answer is yes. Eskimo and others also use a pendulum. This is a string with an object on the end. The shaman asks questions. If the answer is yes, the pendulum swings one way. If it is no, it swings the other way.

Especially in the Americas, shamans use sacred drugs to diagnose illness. The Jívaro shamans of Ecuador drink tobacco water and other sacred plant extracts. They believe they can then see into the patient's body and locate the intruding object.

Dick Mahwee, a Paviotso shaman of Nevada,

describes what he looks for: "I smoke before I go into the trance. . . . I go out [into the spirit world] to see what will happen to the patient. . . . When I see the patient among fresh flowers and he picks them it means that he will recover. If the flowers are withered or look as if the frost had killed them, I know that the patient will die. Sometimes in a trance I see the patient walking on the ground. If he leaves footprints I know that he will live, but if there are no tracks, I cannot cure him."

Sometimes shamans journey to the lower world for information about the illness. In trance, the shaman enters the tunnel to the spirit world. If the patient has a harmful spirit intrusion, the shaman encounters dangerous creatures not far from the entrance—insects or reptiles or fish with large teeth. These creatures are a sign that an object removal is necessary.

Connections Between Shamans and Doctors

The shamans' diagnostic methods may seem bizarre to those who have grown up in a world that believes in science. But there are similarities between the methods of shamans and physicians. Both can be said to enter another reality to make a diagnosis. Medical doctors travel *inside,* to the world of cells and organs. Shamans travel *beyond,* to the world of spirits. Both worlds are hidden from everyday view, from ordinary vision. Both shamans and physicians need "strong eyes" to see this other world. Physicians use the tools and technology that make the microscopic world look bigger. Shamans use their own "strong eye" or divining tools to see the spirit of the illness and predict patients' chances of recovery.

Some shamans even specialize! In many cultures, shamans can cure only particular problems. Australia's Murngin shamans cannot heal soul loss. Willidjungo says that sometimes he looks inside the patient and sees "it's empty" even though the heart

A Western physician dressed in white lab coat uses a stethoscope to detect the presence of disease in her patient's body. Modern healers, not unlike their shaman counterparts, wear special clothing and use special objects in their work.

is still there. Then he says, "I can't fix you up." He tells everybody the patient is going to die.

In Siberia, many shamans can cure only those diseases whose spirits they met during their initiation journey. A shaman who does not have the power to heal a patient may call in another shaman. Anthropologists and medical doctors offer a scientific explanation for this selective ability to heal. They say shamans can safely treat only those diseases to which they have been exposed and become immune. When smallpox was common, for example, Siberian shamans who survived smallpox could treat other smallpox victims without catching the disease. They were considered very powerful. In reality, say some doctors, they were simply immune to the disease.

Healing

After diagnosing the problem, the medical doctors try to prolong physical life by repairing the part of the body that is sick or injured. Shamans try to "nurture and preserve the soul, and to protect it from eternal wandering," according to Jeanne Achterberg.

The shaman may use natural herbal remedies, body work, and other methods common to tribal healers. But shamans use two spiritual healing techniques that set them apart from other healers: They journey to find the lost soul or power. Or they remove the intruder.

Returning the Soul

Shamans in many areas around the world perform ceremonies to return power to sick or injured people. The shaman may first try to call the soul to come back. If it does not respond, the shaman must journey to the spirit world to find it. The shaman may have to contend with enemy spirits and other dangers. Once the shaman locates the soul, he or she hurries back with it and puts it back in the patient.

Old K"xau of Africa describes his journey to re-

An African shaman administers a healing potion to an ill Kenyan woman.

trieve a soul: "If a person dies, I carry him on my back. I lay him out so that we are lying together. . . . That's what I do, my friend. I dance him, dance him, dance him so that God will give his spirit to me. Then I return from God and put his spirit back in his body. My friend, I put it back, put it back, put it back, and that's how he comes out alive."

To the Huichol people of Mexico, loss of soul or the *kupuri* (life force) is a constant danger. Shaman Ramón Medina Silva says the soul lives in the head. When people sleep, the soul can wander. If it is captured by a sorcerer or an animal, the person becomes ill. Or if a person hits his head, the kupuri "falls and is frightened." If the kupuri is not found and returned, the person dies.

The shaman searches for a lost kupuri by listening for it. It is "as small as the smallest insect, the smallest tick," but "it hisses and whispers like a soft wind. . . . [The shaman] goes looking to see where he can hear it," Silva explains, "because the life of that man begins to cry as we cry, as one cries when one is lost, lost far away in the *barranca* [ravine] where one cannot find his way back."

When he locates the whistling soul, the shaman

"The treatment by suction obviously implies sleight-of-hand."

Anthropologist Robert Lowie

"The belief that . . . the shamans' skills were based upon trickery and hallucinations . . . is a failure on the part of the observer to understand the ramifications of differing states of consciousness."

Jeanne Achterberg, medical researcher

whistles back, Silva says, "so that the life can hear him." Then the shaman contacts the Goddess of Children who put life in the patient. The goddess instructs the shaman to pick up the kupuri to protect it from sorcerers and animals. The shaman wraps the kupuri in a wad of cotton and returns to the house where the patient lies. The shaman puts the kupuri with the cotton into the crown of the patient's head. The patient "comes back to life."

In Siberia, South America, Australia, Indonesia, and Malaysia, some shamans use a spirit boat or other craft to travel to the spirit world. The "crew" may be spirits or other shamans. The Coast Salish Indians of Washington State practice an elaborate ritual with the spirit canoe to retrieve the guardian spirit or power animal. A group of six to twelve shamans journey together to the lower world. The shamans stand in two parallel rows. Each shaman has a long pole for paddling. Accompanied by the sounds of rattles, drums, and singing, the shamans' souls paddle to the other world. The land turns into water wherever they travel in the lower world. The ritual lasts two nights or more. At night, the shamans travel in the spirit world. During the day, they rest. Each night, the journey resumes where they left off the night before. When the guardian spirit is retrieved, the shamans return and put it back in the patient.

Sucking or Extraction Technique

Localized pain and aching are often diagnosed as object intrusion. The object is a symbol of a magic spell. Shamans remove the object by sucking it out with their mouths. When they remove the object, they break the spell. The sucking technique is commonly practiced in Siberia, Australia, and North and South America. The shamans suck at the affected part of the body, either through a tube or directly with the mouth. They suck with all their strength. But they are careful not to draw the harmful spirit into their own stomach.

Medical researcher Doug Boyd studied with Rolling Thunder, a North American shaman. In his book *Rolling Thunder,* Boyd tells of the first time he saw the shaman perform a healing ceremony. Several medical doctors also attended.

Rolling Thunder was to heal a young man whose leg had been injured. It was badly infected under the skin. The skin was discolored, swollen, and stretched tight and hard. The pain was so bad the young man could not stand.

Rolling Thunder lit his pipe and drew on it once for each direction he faced—north, south, east, and west. He handed the pipe to his patient who also drew on it four times. Rolling Thunder spoke with the patient briefly. He asked what his plans were

A South African shaman blows herbal powder through a horn into the ear of a sick man as part of a healing ritual.

and why it was important for his leg to be healed. The young man answered that he had important social issues to work on. That seemed to meet with Rolling Thunder's approval. Rolling Thunder began a "high, wailing chant." The sound must have come from Rolling Thunder, Boyd says. Yet "it seemed to come from a point above where he stood."

Then Rolling Thunder sucked at the man's wounded leg. The shaman made "sniffing, howling, and wailing sounds unlike any of the ordinary sounds" people make. After several minutes of sucking, he vomited into a basin that had a piece of raw meat in it. Then he sucked again and vomited again. He did this several times. Twice, he spit into one palm, rubbed his hands together, then placed both hands on the wound. With a feather, Rolling Thunder then made sweeping motions over the patient's entire body. He shook the feather at the raw meat as well.

Rolling Thunder gave instructions that the meat be burned to ashes and that no one should touch it. Then he left. The physicians in the room rushed forward to check the man's leg. The color of his leg had returned to normal. The swelling had gone down. The flesh around the wound was soft. The patient said the pain was gone. A little while later, he was playing an active game of table tennis.

Fraud?

Some witnesses say shamans use sleight of hand to bring about these sucking "miracles." The critics say that shamans go to great lengths to trick the audience. The shaman hides a small object in his or her mouth before the ceremony starts. Then the shaman only pretends to suck it out of the patient's body. One observer said he saw a shaman put red clay in his mouth. When he chewed it, it looked like blood. The ceremony took place in near darkness. The audience was hypnotized by the drumming and chanting, so they believed the shaman was sucking out blood. Another shaman swallowed tobacco to make her nauseous. Then she ate grains of maize. She tied a rope around her waist, which she managed discreetly to pull to induce vomiting. She then claimed she had sucked the maize from the patient's body.

It seems, though, that it is not any secret that the shamans hide objects before the ceremony. Michael Harner explains that this does not take away from the shaman's power in the slightest! The item the shaman sucks merely *stands for* the evil spirit that has invaded the body.

The members of the shaman's own community may know about this "trick." One of the Achomawi people told a researcher, "I don't believe those things come out of the sick man's body. The shaman always has them in his mouth before he starts the treatment. But he draws the sickness into them; he uses them to catch the poison. Otherwise, how could he catch it?"

Psychotherapist?

Shamans are skilled psychotherapists or counselors, some mental health experts say. Their healing ceremonies have great emotional and psychological value.

Their position of authority with the spirits allows them to make strong suggestions for healing. Their presence shifts the patients' attention from the illness to the likelihood of getting better.

"A vital factor in . . . the shaman's healing efforts is in the patient's expectation of being healed," anthropologist Spencer Rogers explains. Shamans do not accept patients they do not think they can heal, Rogers says. So the fact that a shaman has accepted the patient is already a positive sign.

Rogers says shamans use several methods that have a deep psychological effect on the patient during a healing ceremony:

Symbols. Shamans use a medicine bundle, power

A Navajo Indian medicine man sits surrounded by the sacred objects that are the tools of his trade.

objects, a costume, drums, song, and other items to stand for the supernatural. These ancient symbols give patients the idea that powerful and ancient forces are working on their behalf.

Relaxation. Patients are put into a relaxed state by drumming, chanting, massage, and brushing of the body. Patients do not have to do anything but lie back and relax. Relaxation promotes healing.

Hypnosis and suggestion. Hypnosis is an altered state. The steady drumming and chanting can induce this hypnotic state in the patient and the audience. While in this relaxed state, patients are open to the shaman's suggestions. For example, the removal of an object sends a powerful suggestion. It says that the problem has been removed. There is no longer a need to be ill.

Confession. Shamans persuade the patient to confess the sins or broken taboos that might have brought on the illness. The shaman may reenact the painful event. This forces the patient to relive it, deal with it, and then be cleansed of it.

Group support. In many healings, an audience of friends, relatives, and others are present. Patients feel the love and support of the audience. The young man Rolling Thunder treated told a physician that he had been deeply affected by the ceremony. No one had ever paid so much attention to him before. Such deep caring can have a healing effect.

Fraud or Healer?

These methods may be psychologically soothing, but do they bring about physical healing? Some scientists say the shaman "heals" only those people whose illnesses are imagined to begin with. If a physical ailment is cured, it is because the problem ran its natural course anyway.

Some experts believe the shamans' psychological methods are truly helpful. The shamans' methods seem to put patients into an altered state of consciousness which promotes self-healing. People can make themselves sick through stress, worry, anger, and so on. So it may be that people can make themselves well through the power of the mind too. Scientific evidence is mounting that humans have strong healing powers. If that is the case, the shaman's ceremonies may set off the wise "inner healer."

Stanley Krippner is a psychologist and expert on shamanism. He says the shaman Rolling Thunder observes possible patients very carefully, often for many days. He accepts those patients whose "inner healer" is active. He knows then he can work with the inner healer to promote health.

Psychological Explanations

Medical researcher Achterberg suggests that the inner healer involves the imagination. She does not mean "the world of make-believe" when she uses the word *imagination*. Instead she is referring to the realm of *imagery* or mental pictures. Achterberg says shamans teach patients to use imagery to become whole again: "A major cause of both health and sickness, the image is the world's oldest and greatest healing resource." Achterberg says shamans may not do anything that directly changes body chemistry. But their work affects the *imagination*. Because every thought sets off an electrochemical change, imagination can have a profound effect on the body.

Achterberg compares the shamans' work with a modern medical occurrence called the *placebo effect*. The placebo effect is a healing response triggered by a belief or expectation that a treatment will work. Even modern science is not sure *how* it works. But it is clear that the placebo effect does work.

In medical testing, a placebo is a fake drug, such as a sugar pill. One group of patients takes a placebo, but thinks it is a real medicine. Another group takes the real medicine. Then the results are

"The therapeutic effects that the shaman's practices may have are entirely psychological and rest on the suggestibility of the subjects."

Anthropologist S.F. Nadel

"I don't know what you learned from books, but the most important thing I learned from my grandfathers was that there is a part of the mind that we don't really know about and that it is that part that is most important in whether we become sick or remain well."

Thomas Largewhiskers, Navaho medicine man

compared. The testers want to find out whether the medicine truly helps the patients' conditions, or whether the placebo helps just as much. In many tests, the placebos have worked as well as the real medicine. The patients show improvement from taking the placebos because they *think* they are getting medicine. Placebos have helped people with a wide range of conditions—high blood pressure, arthritis, cancer, acne, multiple sclerosis, diabetes, allergies, and depression, for example.

Achterberg says the shamans' work is a placebo. Like the patients taking sugar pills, the shamans' patients *think* the treatment will work. The patients start to see themselves being healed or getting relief for their pain. The *image*-ination has started working. On the other hand, if a patient thought the treatment were harmful, it could have a negative effect. The body's processes change depending upon what the mind expects will happen.

"The placebo is actually granting permission to heal," Achterberg says. That may also be what the shaman is doing—granting the patient permission to heal.

Physician and philosopher Roger Walsh says the shaman's "tricks and sleight of hand" encourage healing. They increase faith in the shaman's power. They increase the expectation of being healed. Walsh writes, "Clearly the placebo effect has been one of the most powerful forces for healing throughout human history. . . . Shamans may have been the first to harness it systematically."

Shamanic Methods in Modern Treatment

Today, medical doctors are openly urging patients to use their imaginations for healing. They are tapping the "mind/body" connection to search for methods to heal AIDS, cancer, and other life-threatening illnesses.

Dr. Bernie Siegel, a surgeon and cancer specialist, believes very strongly in the importance of the mind in healing. He says medical treatment works best when patients use their emotions and imagery to promote healing: "These are the two ways we can get our minds and bodies to communicate with each other. Our emotions and words let the body know what we expect of it, and by visualizing certain changes we can help the body bring them about." Siegel's patients visualize tumors shrinking and disappearing. They picture their cancer cells being eaten up by white blood cells. They also address the emotional problems that sap their energy. These problems are robbing them of power!

Some would say that Siegel and other doctors are urging their patients to be their own "shamans." They have adopted the shamans' view of health as *wholeness* of body and spirit. Disease is a sign that there is an emotional or spiritual imbalance. Healing can only come about when patients deal with these imbalances in relationships, work, and so on. Healing does not necessarily mean that the patient will not die of the disease. But healing will bring emotional and spiritual peace. It will improve the quality of the patient's remaining days.

There is still a wide gap, however, in the views of why shamans' ways work. The physician or psychologist might say that shamans are masters of hypnosis and suggestion. They provide patients with hope. They teach patients to use their minds for healing themselves.

To the shaman, however, the supernatural is at work. Maybe the spirits work through the mind. Maybe they work through the body. But they are at work restoring the patient's power.

American medical doctor Bernie Siegel teaches his patients to help heal their bodies by visualizing wellness and expressing positive emotions.

Afterword

Shamanism in the Modern World

(opposite page) Atlanta storeowner Betty Moss displays some of the crystals she sells. Many people report improved health and increased spiritual power using certain mineral crystals.

Shamanism used to be a subject mainly for anthropologists and religion historians. It was considered to belong mostly to the past and to a few simple cultures around the world. But in recent years, interest in shamanism has increased. People living in modern societies are finding much of value in shamanic beliefs and practices. Shamanic teachings are changing people's attitudes about personal healing and the healing of the earth.

Shaman and anthropologist Michael Harner says that shamanism answers a hunger for the spiritual in the modern world. Modern people are out of balance because they have neglected their spiritual nature. This imbalance has had serious effects on people and on the planet.

Shamanism reawakens a sense of mystery, a sense that there is more to the world than meets the eye. Shamanic methods can teach people to use the hidden powers of the mind to experience the power and energy of the universe. Harner says that practicing shamanic methods can open people up to a world of beauty, harmony, balance, and wisdom.

He also states that everyone has shamanic abilities. Harner teaches people around the world how to awaken those abilities. He says that most people

learn to journey very easily.

Harner's methods involve the use of the shamanic drum. Students relax in a dark room with their eyes closed. While the drummer beats steadily, the students picture an entrance to an underground tunnel that takes them into the earth. They pass through the tunnel and enter the other world. There they meet a guide who shows them around this other world. A change in the beat of the drum calls them back to ordinary reality.

Students learn to use journeying to seek answers to questions for themselves and others. They learn to travel to the other world to help heal others by bringing back a power animal, says Harner. By healing others, people also heal themselves. They maintain their own power and health by drawing on the power of the universe to help others.

Teacher and shaman Brooke Medicine Eagle also believes that shamanic work can restore balance. She says, "We must awaken to the spirit that is in every one of our cells and the power that lives in everything." Like Harner, she believes we must "touch and unfold our shamanic will . . . to find our power."

In shamanism, power is not power *over* something or someone. Power is the force or energy that gives people life and health. Health is balance. According to shamanic belief, illness is caused by a loss of power. Something in one's life is out of balance. Power—health—is leaking away. To restore health, one must restore power by finding balance again.

Listening to the Inner Voice

Whether or not people believe in the mystical powers of shamanism, they can learn certain practical things from this ancient belief system. Shamanic practice can teach people to listen to the inner voice, the voice of the spirits. That is, it teaches people to find their own way, to be true to themselves spiritually. Shamans become sick when they resist shamanizing. They become powerful when

A New York trash dump overflows into the harbor. If more people today shared the shaman's attitude that the land, rivers, and oceans are living things, perhaps humans would respect rather than abuse the environment.

they accept the call of the spirit. The shamans' lesson is to follow one's calling. If people are not true to their calling, they too lose their power. They become out of balance. The shaman is calling people to respect their own inner voices and to find their own power.

Shamanism also speaks strongly to people's concerns about the fate of the planet. The earth is threatened by pollution, garbage, the ozone layer, nuclear waste, and many other dangers. Shamanism teaches respect for the earth. Shamanic people belive that all of nature is alive and full of energy. All of nature is interconnected and related. Trees, mountains, birds, fish, rocks, lakes, and people are all relatives. If one part is out of balance, then the entire system is out of balance. The well-being of people and the well-being of the planet are connected. Humans cannot be healthy and balanced while the earth and its other beings are sick.

Through shamanism, Michael Harner says, people can learn to talk to the plants and animals as our ancestors did. He believes this may save the planet. He points out that our ancestors talked to nature for three million years and the earth survived very well. But in our world, "where people *don't* talk with the planet and its inhabitants," we face nuclear and environmental disaster.

Shamanism teaches that no one being can rule or dominate nature. There is no balance while one person or thing dominates and tries to suppress the power of other beings.

Learning to journey does not make a person a shaman in the sense discussed in this book. But following shamanic beliefs does foster wonder and respect towards the earth, a sense of inner power, and a commitment to helping other people. We can help heal the planet and ourselves by honoring all things, in the shamanic tradition.

For Further Exploration

Jeanne Achterberg, *Imagery in Healing, Shamanism and Modern Medicine*. Boston, MA: New Science Library, Shambhala Publications, Inc., 1985.

Doug Boyd, *Rolling Thunder*. New York: Random House, 1974.

Gary Doore, ed., *Shaman's Path*. Boston, MA: Shambhala Publications, Inc., 1988.

Mircea Eliade, *Shamanism*. Princeton, NJ: Princeton University Press, 1964.

Joan Halifax, *Shaman, The Wounded Healer*. London: Thames and Hudson, Ltd., 1982.

Joan Halifax, *Shamanic Voices*. New York: E.P. Dutton, 1979.

Michael Harner, *The Way of the Shaman, A Guide to Power and Healing*. New York: Bantam Books, 1980.

Michele Jamal, *Shape Shifters*. New York and London: Arkana, 1987.

Holger Kalweit, *Dreamtime and Inner Space*. Boston, MA: Shambhala Publications, Inc., 1984.

Stephen Larsen, *The Shaman's Doorway*. New York: Harper and Row, 1976.

W.A. Lessa and E.Z. Vogt, *Reader in Comparative Religion*. New York: Harper and Row, 1972.

John G. Neihardt, *Black Elk Speaks*. Lincoln, NE: University of Nebraska Press, 1961.

Shirley Nicholson, ed., *Shamanism*. Wheaton, IL: Quest Books, The Theosophical Publishing House, 1987.

Michael Talbot, *Beyond the Quantum*. New York and Toronto: Bantam Books, 1986.

Roger Walsh, *The Spirit of Shamanism*. Los Angeles: Jeremy Tarcher, Inc., 1990.

Index

About the Author

Wendy Stein, a free-lance writer and editor, lives in Syracuse, New York. She has written and edited materials on a variety of subjects, including health, social studies, history, consumer education, and communication skills. Her recent books include *Great Mysteries: Atlantis* and *Ready, Set, Study*.

She earned a B.A. in English and religion from Trinity College in Hartford, Connecticut, and an M.A. in public communications from Syracuse University.

She enjoys camping, canoeing, cross-country skiing, whale-watching, and an occasional risk such as rock-climbing or fire-walking.

Picture Credits